Great Masters of Scottish Football

HUGH TAYLOR

Great Masters
of Scottish Football

STANLEY PAUL *London*

STANLEY PAUL & CO LTD
178–202 Great Portland Street, London W1

AN IMPRINT OF THE   HUTCHINSON GROUP

London Melbourne Sydney
Auckland Bombay Toronto
Johannesburg New York

★

First published 1967

*This book has been set in Garamond, printed in Great Britain
on Antique Wove paper by Anchor Press, and
bound by Wm. Brendon, both of Tiptree, Essex*

Contents

Illustrations

I

The Old—or the New?

THE jet age has brought a revolution to football. It has not been a universally popular change. But, whether we like it or not, the new conception of a game that had remained, in rules and tactics, stubbornly conservative for almost half a century is here to stay. Those who feel excitement has departed with the expulsion of high crosses, W-formations and full-blooded sorties by burly centre-forwards are as out of date as a rosy-cheeked squire sighing for a four-in-hand to replace his Bentley.

The accent now is on method, on discipline, and when you see kids at play on a village green trying to use a 4—2—4 formation and arguing about who is to be 'sweeper' you realise that there is no use sighing for the past.

There must be progress, no matter how much some of us abhor change in our favourite sport.

What is the new style?

It is not just merely a matter of numbers. There have been many changes, but the most important is that today we are in the age of the all-purpose player.

No longer is soccer an individual's game, with players left to play 'be ear', as it were. It is much more of a team affair, entirely different to that played in the past when a winger was a winger and a full-back a full-back and woe betide him if he ventured into his opponents' half of the field.

Although football has changed, the reaction of the experts, never mind the fans, hasn't. Bitter argument rages over the new style.

For instance, Dr. Percy M. Young, the most amiable, erudite and imaginative writer football has known, says the type of game being played today puts it among the fine arts. Football, he feels, has reached a renaissance point, thanks to a new fluency springing from the union of old and more recent styles, extra licence given to artistry and a greater capacity for improvisation. The game, he enthuses, is becoming almost exotic.

On the other hand, Alfredo di Stefano, about whose expert knowledge there can be no disagreement because he was, when with Real Madrid, one of world's outstanding footballers, declares the new style is taking the beauty out of the game. Although technique, training and tactical plans have improved, there are fewer stars, he says, and too many teams are playing defensively.

And Pele, the Brazilian who has been the world's favourite player since 1958, is equally distressed. Of the 1966 World Cup competition in England, the series that put the seal on the new method football, the football that brought the highest success, he said frankly: 'It looks as though brutality pays. Running with the ball, I found as never before that my calculations were disturbed not by fears of a hard legal tackle, for that's in the game, but by thoughts that I had certain opponents whose chief aim was to disable me.'

Who's right? I know better than to try to be the arbitrator in any football argument. My own view, though, is that too many people are trying to make the game an exact science, and when football becomes mass-produced, no matter how gleamingly perfect, much of the excitement vanishes. Yet Celtic, who play football in a style as up-to-date as tomorrow's headlines, have proved that the game of the 1960's can be as exciting, as explosive, as any ever played in the past. Much depends on the team manager. Some are content to rely on defence, on dull but effective 4—2—4's or 4—3—3's. But Celtic's manager, Jock Stein, realises that to attract the crowds there must be gaiety about the game and he has wisely recognised that a plan cannot be an end in itself and he believes in attacking football.

No matter what we think of modern football, there is one aspect about which there can be no argument: it is tougher than it ever was; the spirit of adventure is going out; the formula is becoming all; and, I'm sorely afraid, the day of the individual master of the game is drawing to a close.

How formidable are the obstacles that confront an aspiring James, Morton, Gallacher, Mason, Buchan, Smith, Matthews, Doherty, Finney, Templeton, Meredith, Dunne or Jackson today.

The hopes of an aspiring football genius are quenched, first, by the highly engineered precision play which has become the style nearly all over the world, play in which every man is no more than a unit, though a skilled unit, I must admit.

The mathematical approach is killing the brilliant individualist, although I must, in fairness, say that modern football taxes the ingenuity of the player where formerly it was his physical strength that carried the strain. But there is no doubt that the fluidity of current strategy—and I refer to the best of modern methods—eliminates the clear-cut specialisation of earlier times.

But I must be blunt. The real reason many of the great masters of the game wouldn't live in it nowadays is that they'd be chopped out of it. Di Stefano sums it up sadly: 'The objective in too many cases today is to stop others from playing—not to play themselves.' This is the day of the destroyer.

Football has become more violent, reeking of the jungle or the gladiatorial arena of old Rome. Some may like it this hot and say that the old-timers weren't fit enough or strong enough to be aces today. I may be old-fashioned—but I preferred the artistry of yesterday to the attrition of today.

So this may be a book for the sentimentalists like myself. There are many of us, I know. Whether we are right to look back on the past so often through the rosy glow of retrospect is a matter only for ourselves to ponder.

We may be anachronisms. Our fondness for the suavity and grace of the men of arts and parts—which contrasted so bizarrely with their embarrassingly cumbersome equipment of iron-toed boots, laces that would have tied a liner securely to dock, long-john pants, shinguards that turned legs into supports for a billiards-table and jerseys as old-fashioned as grannie's bathing costume—may be laughed to scorn by the 'mod' athletes of today, so arrogantly *soigné* and energetic and 'with it' in footwear as supple as an Indian's hunting moccasin and a strip as superbly designed for the job as the holster for a Colt revolver.

It is wrong, however, to say that all the players of the past who gave us so much pleasure would be out of place in the football of today. There were some whose presence on the field—we are not at all unhappy to say, with a gleam of unholy joy in our eye—who would have had the modern hired assassins, sinister if skilful destroyers, running for their lives. For they were more powerful, more able than the alleged 'hard men' of today to dish out punishment if they had to.

We must not forget that since football began there have been tough guys—but some toughs were also masters of the game, players who had that certain something, that style to make them stand out from their fellows. It takes all kinds to make a football team, remember.

And we still have the power boys—and they are luckier than their predecessors because football pattern now suits their talents ideally.

Disappearing, however, is the type of player who was once symbolic of the artistry of Scottish soccer. To him flair was all. The shrug of the shoulders, the flick of the hip, the dummy, the careful precision pass, the oily swerve—these were his weapons and how well he used them. He was usually an inside-forward, though not necessarily so. He was a specialist in altruism. His job was to make goals, not score them, to hold the ball for the fraction of a second needed for his younger and more virile colleagues to take up position, then slide the ball to the man most likely to be able to shoot without distraction. This type was an individualist—and I loved him.

He was master of the ball and, like a true craftsman, he wanted time to caress his love. Football to him was pure enjoyment. But the method play of the 1960's would be anathema.

From players of this type, however, most of Scotland's greatness in the game sprung. The true father of the distinctively Scottish type of inside-forward play was Bobby Walker, of Heart of Midlothian, who had twenty-nine full international caps for Scotland. He wasn't fast. But no one had quicker mental agility; no one had his power of deluding opponents.

I wish I had seen him. Alas, he was before my time. But I saw his successors. There were many—players such as Jimmy Mason, Jimmy Williamson, Willie Buchan, Tommy Walker, Willie Mills, players to whom art was all.

This was the type of player, essentially Scottish, who, I'm afraid, would find the game a sad disappointment now. There is little scope for the player who liked to stop and think, to dally with the ball, secure in the knowledge that his educated feet could flick it delicately away from lunging tackles.

And I have the feeling the pace and close marking of present-day football would have ruined the magic of the men who were the real craftsmen of the Scottish game.

It's only a feeling, mark you. For we who look back so nostalgically to the past are apt to forget that football has always had its quota of players who weren't afraid to present their power. And the stars with the velvet touch shone against backs certainly brawnier and rasher than those of today.

We must remember, too, that the great fascination of Scottish football has always been its variety—variety in style of play and in type of player. It took all types to make Scottish football great. There were rough players and gentle players; there were saints and sinners; there was, most of all, the great attraction of opposites. That's the essence of all drama and that's why Scottish football was such superb entertainment.

We may, for instance, bawl fiercely at a burly back who is digging into a wisp of a winger and we may be contemptuous of a team which relies purely on defence, especially if our own club pins its faith on bright, attacking football—but how we relish the battle of wits when the opposites meet.

Yes, opposites—that has probably been the secret of any success we've had in football. Remember Stevenson and Ferrier? There has never been a better wing partnership than that of the Motherwell pair in the 'thirties—George Stevenson with his superb skill, magical use of the open space and perfect passes, and Bobby Ferrier with his booming shot, direct thrusts and ability to be in exactly the right place to make best use of his partner's passes.

In Scotland the true art of football is to blend players, to allow them to play naturally, whether skilfully or robustly.

So perhaps I am doing my favourites, the artists, the tanner ba' experts, the real entertainers, an injustice. Perhaps they would have been as outstanding now as they were in their heyday. Perhaps they would have fitted perfectly into our modern systems.

We will never know, for we can never compare, argue as we will, the idols of yesterday with those of today, for styles have changed, there is a new conception of training and, undoubtedly, the pace of football has quickened.

Probably the truth is that some of the old-timers would be just as impressive if they were playing today—and some of our outstanding players of the 1960's would still have become legends if they had been playing years ago.

It's a matter of personal choice, which, after all, is one of the most fascinating aspects of football, for controversy is the lifeblood of the game.

I have made these points, tried to illustrate the vividly contrasting styles of play and players and presented the conflicting views of eminent critics in order to show the difficulties confronting anyone who has the temerity to make a list of the great masters of Scottish football.

Please remember it's only my selection. You may not agree. Indeed, I'm sure you won't. And you are as much entitled to your opinion as I am. That, as I've said, is the delight of football. In this country we are so much involved in football that the view of the spectator on the terracing is often as correct as that of the player, manager or writer.

What has worried me most is in trying to decide just who should be called a great master of Scottish football. Should the appellation be given only to an architect of a forward line, an artist, a schemer, a thinker? As I've said, my favourite players have been men in this mould. But there have been, and still are, wonderful players whose attributes have been power, pace, perseverance. They have added colour and gaiety and excitement to football and are entitled to be included in the game's hall of fame.

Of course, when you think of a master you think first of all of style. But is style all? Certainly not. Take golf. Some of the great masters of that difficult game have been players with classical swings. But few of the top golfers of today, Nicklaus, Player, Palmer, can be called stylists; to them power is all. And have there ever been more successful golfers than this trio?

I went to the dictionary. I was as bewildered as ever. For I found a master means many things, including: a man who rules; a director; a teacher; an appellation given to a boy; the chief of a society. I also found that master can mean an appellation of respect. And that is the one for me.

The masters I have named in this book are players for whom I have had the greatest respect. Some are dead. Some are still stars. Some relied on intuition. Some could have been illustrations for a textbook on how the game should be played. Some were eccentric. Some were forwards, some defenders. But every one, I insist, was—or is—a great master of football. They had one thing in common: despite the differences in physique, in style, in position, in outlook to the game, they were masters of the ball.

If I have missed out your particular favourite I'm sorry. I may even be wrong in not naming him. But in a book of this kind the choice must be strictly personal. And I can only hope memories as fond as mine will be evoked for many of you in some of my selections.

2

Alex James—King of them All

IT IS of inside-forwards that the Scottish troubadours sing and the heroic tales are told. The supreme inside-rights and -lefts have always captured the eye and gripped the imagination of the fans to a greater extent than players in any other position on the field. You might think that the centre-forwards, the players who usually put the finishing touch to great feats of team-work, were the players best remembered by the crowds trudging home to their high teas. Not in Scotland. The inside-man is the player held in highest esteem.

The reason for this, I believe, lies in the average Scot's respect for craftsmanship. And the inside-forward is the engineer of the team. It is to true to say that while there is always the flamboyant character whose dearest dream is to score the winning goal for Scotland at Hampden the majority of football enthusiasts in this country would rather be inside-forwards. And certainly no footballing nation has been so rich in genius in this position as Scotland.

You cannot, of course, assert that the Scottish inside-forwards emerged from the same conveyor belt, that they all played alike. You could never compare Bobby Walker with Billy Steel, Jimmy Mason with Bob McPhail. Some were more devastating scorers than others.

But at the heart of their play was the same beat. They were all masters of design. Even those of baroque genius, even those whose principal asset was a spectacular burst through a bewildered defence, were essentially builders. Like a Clyde-side engineer, they pinned their faith in stout construction, a distinctive touch and true Scottish craft. They were all pains-taking in their efforts to make their teams flow. They knew they were the mainsprings, knew they were the men whose main job was to construct the pads from which the missiles flew. They did their task superbly. A few still do, even in the football revolution.

Which inside-forward is most deserving of a stained-glass window? Celtic friends continue to tell me that undoubtedly the greatest inside-forward was Patsy Gallacher and I respect their judgment. Certainly Bobby Walker must come into the lists. For me, however, there can be only Alex James. As far as I am concerned, he was king of them all, the player I idol-ised, the greatest inside-forward I ever knew.

And I must at once reply to the moderns who, pointing to this age of the all-purpose player, allege that while James may have reigned supreme in his day he could never have been so outstanding today because he was merely a provider and never a taker of goals. This is nonsense. Alex James was one of the most versatile of inside-forwards.

Indeed, he could have been remembered as a prince of scorers and it was a long time before he settled down with Arsenal because, until he was transferred from Preston to the Highbury club in 1929—for £9,000, imagine it!—he had scored goals galore and he wasn't happy when it was made clear to him that his new job was to make goals, to go back and help the defenders and create opportunities for goals for David Halliday, the Scottish centre-forward from Sunder-land.

That role, however, he finally adopted—and that made his name.

What was the secret of James, a small, bullet-headed chatterbox, who always wore long, flapping shorts that were the delight of the cartoonists, the centre parting that was the trade-mark of so many Scottish sporting heroes of the 'twenties and 'thirties, and buttoned sleeves?

He worked miracles of sleight-of-foot. He had uncanny anticipation. His passing was incredibly accurate.

But Denzil Batchelor, the distinguished author, summed it up best thus: 'If you must compare James with some past master out of another world of sport, Jimmy Wilde is the nearest parallel to suggest itself. Wilde the boxer had that quality which particularly distinguished James: the gift of absence at the precise moment when the massed attack went in at its strongest.'

In naming Alex James the greatest inside-forward in Scottish football history I can be accused, I must admit, of bias. James, for instance, was supreme in his sphere in an era which to me was glittering, the early 'thirties, when life was bubbling over and there was a call for young men to get up and go in the mellow voice of Crosby and the haunting horn of Beiderbecke and no lights were brighter than those of London and Fleet Street was a street of adventure and it was good to know that young Scots like James and Gallacher and Jackson could join in the jinks of high society because they were stars in their own right.

I am biased, too, because I became a friend of Alex James and I know kindliness abounded in that small frame.

Although I had seen him play and became more entranced every time he fluttered his foot over the ball as if about to back-heel it, stopping tacklers bearing down on him in their very tracks, I had never met Alex James until shortly after the war.

It was my first international. I was reporting a Wales-Scotland match at Wrexham. I was raw and nervous and in awe of famous colleagues. Hesitantly I ventured into the bar of my hotel, where practically every official in the game and writer was staying, bought a drink and sat in a corner.

Suddenly a thickset figure appeared before me. 'Hey, son' —and the accent was guid Scots tinged with London—'what paper do you work for?' I told him. 'Never met you before,' said Alex James, 'but don't sit there by yourself. Come and join us.'

And he took me over to his group, introduced me to famed reporters and managers and, indeed, gave me a start in foot-ball-writing that aspiring journalists dream about. Because if Alex James introduced you you were really in in football.

At the match it was James who said, 'Use mine,' when my telephone packed up and that evening it was James who took me in and regaled me with his fund of football anecdotes, although he was interrupted nearly every five minutes by someone coming up to shake his hand or ask for his autograph.

Personal feelings aside, I am not alone in my conviction that Alex was the king of them. The former Arsenal manager, George Allison, has declared: 'Alex was the greatest expo-nent of all the arts and crafts known to Association football.' Colleagues of James have told me the same thing.

Unlike some players for whom 'Yes' and 'No' are an excess of conversation, Alex was a wonderful talker, both on and off the field, and one of the most delightful stories told of him was related gleefully by Jimmy McMullan, captain of the Wembley Wizards team. After that memorable match he was asked by a sportswriter if there had been a plan to beat Eng-land. Jimmy grinned and said: 'Aye, we laid down a plan. It was a simple one but a stern one. I told the boys: "Now I don't want any unnecessary talking. Get on with the game and don't talk to opponents or referee." '

The awed reporter said: 'That was good. Certainly it

worked.' McMullan replied: 'Did it heck! Alex James's tongue went like a gramophone from the kick-off.' The reporter asked: 'Did you tick him off?' 'Don't be daft,' said Jimmy. 'How could I? If his tongue went like a gramophone, so did his feet.'

It's true that Alex James wasn't always the level-headed Scot and the impish mischief of his play was sometimes reflected off the field. Once when Preston North End were in special training at Matlock before a cup-tie, passers-by in the main street turned to stare at an extraordinary figure. There was a dapper young man, wearing a bowler hat, plus-fours, white spats over a pair of patent-leather shoes, canary-coloured gloves and an unrolled umbrella. It was, of course, Alex James, startling the staid inhabitants of the health resort to win a bet from a colleague.

Although he was known as a humorist, bubbling over with the joy of life, Alex also revelled in the battle of football. Like all great players, his will to win was tremendous and he could be furious with colleagues who failed to respond to his urging. It has been said that he had a capacity for perplexing not only foe but also friend, but that was not to be wondered at, for I have never seen a player with such a quick brain, with such a flair for spotting an opening and he was often two moves ahead of his mates, which, naturally, often led to confusion.

Alex James was born in 1902 at Mossend, near Glasgow, and he used to joke that he was born with a football in his mouth, which wasn't far from the truth, for, like most of his friends in the little mining village, he was kicking a ball around almost as soon as he could walk.

Soon it was apparent that James was going to be a footballing genius and as he played for local clubs his fame spread. He worked as a clerk in a local steelworks and he formed a friendship with Hughie Gallacher, destined to lead Scotland to many famous victories. These two were known as 'The Inseparables' and they were side by side in the Wembley Wizards eleven in 1928.

They had, incidentally, only one thing in common—their love of football and their ability to play it. For psychologically the men were poles apart. James was a friendly extrovert. Gallacher, though his tongue, like Alex's, could flick like a serpent's, was more withdrawn, more intense, yet more liable to blow his top. They were, however, firm friends and their play benefited because of it.

Certainly as boys their genius flourished with a string-tied ball as equipment and brave hearts that strove for perfection. No one could ever doubt their courage, and all too often, both as boys and men, big bruises were their medals.

All too soon James and Gallacher parted company and, after playing for the Glasgow junior club Asfield, Alex graduated to Raith Rovers in 1922, was transferred to Preston for £3,275 in 1925 and reached his zenith when he went to Arsenal for £9,000 in 1929.

Fame, however, did not come immediately. As has happened so often, a player, no matter how brilliant, does not always immediately settle with a new club and often at the start of his career at Highbury he wondered just why there had been angry outbursts from the fans of the club he had left.

There was a story that when a politician addressed a meeting in Preston he happened to mention a statesman whose first name was James and added: 'James was worth his weight in gold.' At once a member of the audience asked: 'Can the candidate tell us if America has offered the war debt for Alex James?' A voice cut in: 'They couldn't have him if they offered us America.'

Although James did not suffer from false modesty, he was anything but big-headed and he began to have serious doubts about his ability to perform the new role to which he had been assigned. He had always relished being a goal-scorer and liked to play well upfield. Now he was being asked to be the distributor-in-chief and his whole way of football life was changed. He wasn't sure, either, whether he could put up with the dictatorial attitude of Herbert Chapman.

Appointed manager of Arsenal in 1925, Chapman became the supreme name in Arsenal history, the iron man of the club. He ran the club as Bill Struth ran Rangers, as Willie Maley ran Celtic—the supremo, the commander-in-chief who would stand no nonsense from anyone, office boy, player or director.

Alex had never met anyone like him and, at first, there were clashes. Chapman had evolved new tactics following the new rule which reduced the number of defenders who could put a man offside from three to two. The basis of the plan was to keep control of the mid-field, making the centre-half into a third back; the wing-halves no longer glued themselves to the opposing wingers but had to drop back to assist their backs when the other team swung into attack; and the raiding party consisted of flying wingers, a bustling centre-forward and inside-forwards who were rovers, picking up clearances to switch the side into attack.

Does that remind you of present-day method tactics? There's nothing much new in football.

Then Chapman decided one inside-forward should play further up, alongside the centre-forward; his main job was to engineer shooting opportunities for him. That role fell to David Jack, who had a notable body swerve and also a fierce shot.

This meant the other inside-forward had to play even further back and Alex thought he and Jack should switch roles. Chapman didn't. As always, Chapman won. And, as inevitably as night follows day, Chapman was right.

'I've never known Herbert wrong,' Alex once admitted to me. 'I had my rows with him but there was no greater manager in football.'

James was finally dropped, then recalled—to perform the role Chapman had allotted him. By now Alex knew there was nothing for it but to try his best. He decided that if Chapman considered he was the best man available for the tricky task of rover then Chapman was right—and he might as well become James the prince of goal-makers as James the ace of goal-snatchers.

In the Cup Final of 1930 the Arsenal attack was Hulme, Jack, Lambert, James and Cliff Bastin. Arsenal beat Huddersfield Town 2—0. It was James who clinched the game with a goal that reflected his genius. Not only did he make it; he scored it. Arsenal were awarded a free kick. Huddersfield relaxed for a moment as they took up defensive positions. But James had already summed up the situation. He had been the player fouled. He got up, instantly glanced at the referee, got a wave of consent, flicked a pass to Bastin, shouted for the ball to be given back at once, gathered the return and sent the ball into the net—all before the Town players realised what had happened.

James became the idol of Highbury. The crowd would chant 'James! James! James!' as the 5 ft. 6 in. morsel cavorted gaily, the ball seemingly tied to his bootlaces and with a nonchalance that was almost cheek.

Like every great player, Alex was a showman, which was probably the reason for his famous trademark, the long pants which flapped well below his knees. Why did he wear them? As a distinguishing feature by which he could be identified by colleagues? Alex always laughed when I asked him and said: 'The reason was simpler than that. The pants kept my knees warm on a cold day.'

James would have been just as supreme in present-day football. He would have stood out, as Jim Baxter does, in the efficient method game. He would have been a terror to packed defences because his long pass was immaculate. He might, however, have had harsh words to say about the emphasis on defence, just as he had when he first arrived at Highbury. But he was the complete professional and in the end he would have done what his manager asked—and done it in his own inimitable way.

Honours fell thick on James. He was capped eight times for Scotland and from 1929 until his retirement in 1937 he helped Arsenal to win the F.A. Cup twice and the League championship four times. In this modern era he would never have been out of the Scotland team.

How would James have stood up to the pace, the close marking of today? I'm convinced it wouldn't have worried him. He was the target for abuse in his playing days and Arsenal trainer Tom Whittaker once said: 'Alex should have been one footballer who ought to have worn shinguards on the backs of his legs rather than the fronts.' His uncanny body swerve and feint were such that his back was more often turned to an opponent than his front, and rivals, trying to get the ball away, repeatedly damaged the calves of his legs. It never worried Alex. He always tried to get on with the game and, unlike some sharper-tempered Scottish colleagues of his day, he seldom retaliated. 'I was too wee to fight,' he often told me.

Although he was never a prima donna, Alex James had his dignity and when he was outraged he refused to be comforted.

In 1933 it was his duty as team captain to receive the English League Championship token on behalf of Arsenal at a
gathering of England's soccer greats. When dinner was
served, however, there was no Alex James to grace the table.
He was at home, his pride wounded, desperately hurt because
he had been dropped from the last match of the season. And
once even the formidable Chapman, whom James came to
admire so greatly, could not persuade him to re-sign for the
club. Alex stood out for months because of a grievance. Then
for probably the first time in his aloof managerial life Mr.
Chapman lost his temper. He heard over the telephone that
James had signed—for Selfridges. The independent wee Scot
had joined that London store as a sports demonstrator.

Alex always had a hankering to be a businessman. Alas, he
was never as successful there as he was as a footballer. He was
a director of a football pools firm, owner of a sweets-and-
tobacco shop, a pig farmer—and, of all things, director of a
women's outfitters in Aylesbury. He was much happier when
he began writing football for a Sunday newspaper.

His friendliness was legendary. Everyone liked the wee
Scot with the big grin, the blob of a pert nose and the heart
of gold. All football mourned when he died in 1953.

Alex was an entrancing storyteller—but his best story concerned the greatest day of his football life: that wonderful
day of March 31st, 1928, when he played for the Wembley
Wizards.

Those of you who are too young to remember the Wizards,
probably the greatest Scottish international team ever fielded,
would have enjoyed Alex's pawky comments on the match.

'Never before,' said Alex, 'had a team been so severely
panned by the critics. Our team was said to be too small up
front. We were given no chance but we were never really
discouraged.' His face creased into the wrinkled grin that

was so endearing. 'You know what I mean, Hugh. We knew what you reporters wrote. We always felt the opposite would happen. No offence.

'Anyhow, it rained just before the game so the Wembley pitch was treacherous. But it suited our short, on-the-ground Scottish play. We small chaps kept the ball down, never giving the defenders time to recover, and we also marked the English forwards closely.

'I often wondered, though, what would have happened if England had scored in the first minute, as they almost did. Billy Smith, the Huddersfield left-winger, slipped past Nelson and closed in to beat Jack Harkness with a terrific drive. The ball hit the post and Jack had a lot to do with that, for he had narrowed the angle for Smith, the best he could do.

'Two minutes after that escape we were a goal up. McMullan pushed the ball to Gibson, back it came to me, through to Alan Morton and there was Alex Jackson to head home a centre from the left. Not an Englishman touched the ball while we made that wonderful goal.'

Alex loved to recount the Wizards story. He had been the hero of countless football battles but never, he told me, had he been so excited about any match as that Wembley clash of so long ago. He always felt, too, that the greatest goal he ever scored was Scotland's second in that match.

'It was nearly half-time. As Wilson, the English centre-half, came at me, I feinted, half-turned and cracked a volley from twenty-five yards. I had a feeling about that shot. I knew Ted Hufton in the England goal would never get near it. And he didn't.'

I once asked Alex what was the real secret of the Wizards, the men who won 5—1 and became football immortals. He smiled that comic's grin of his and said: 'Looking back, I think it was the audacious confidence of Jackson and the determination of Hughie Gallacher that gave us the inspiration we needed.

'Just before the match—there were no lengthy get-togethers of players before an international in those days—I went to pick up Alec Jackson, who was visiting his Huddersfield club-mates, Smith, Wilson, Goodall and Kelly, at their hotel.

'And what do you think the bold Alec was doing? He was telling his mates, who were to play against him at Wembley, how he was going to crack the goals in that afternoon and how we were going to lick the pants off them. No half-measures about Alec. He scored three goals.'

James scored two goals—for this was in the days when he was noted as a marksman. Afterwards he became famous as a distributor-in-chief. But he always had the mark of greatness. He was brilliantly versatile, this wee man in the baggy pants, who, like all great players, was a showman.

He was the best inside-forward I ever saw.

3

Flash of Steel

HE HAD steel springs for muscles, a choirboy's face that masked a devouring, often ruthless, determination to achieve football perfection, a caustic tongue that frequently angered team-mates more bitterly than opponents and a style and ability that, in this modern age, would have had the wealthy clubs of Europe bidding frantically for his transfer.

Billy Steel was the first of what can be termed the international jet set of players. He would have been a success, though he might not have been idolised, with Inter-Milan or Real Madrid, Chelsea or Celtic, Penorol or Santos.

Unlike so many of his predecessors who were indelibly stamped with the style of their birthplace, Steel was classless. No one watching this chirpy little man in action could have said from which soccer school he graduated. About Bobby Walker, Tommy McInally, Jimmy Mason, Bobby Johnstone, there was something essentially Scottish. Where else but in England, for instance, could Steve Bloomer, Charlie Buchan, Stan Cullis or Billy Wright have been born?

Steel was different. Steel belonged to the élite corps of players—the corps that includes Di Stefano, Pele, Puskas, Law, Suarez, Rivera, Kopa, Orcwirk, Seeler: the global greats.

What was his secret? It was that of Denis Law's: an agile brain, a puma's pounce and extraordinary gymnastic ability that put him invariably a move ahead of his colleagues. There was nothing svelte about Steel; he exuded vitality, he had the killer instinct of a boxing champion, he was the type of aggressive attacker who was so keen to win that he would have sworn at his best friend if he felt he hadn't been pulling his weight.

I recall a famous Hibernian player telling me how surprised he had been when Steel suddenly turned to him in a match in which Dundee were chasing the Scottish First Division championship and snarled: 'How would you like to play with a bunch of mugs like that every Saturday?'

That was Steel. He had been playing his heart out, as usual, and his blood was up and he couldn't stop his tongue wagging.

And there was an occasion in an international match when, coming off the field at half-time, he snarled at a colleague: 'You'd be better keeping up with play than combing your hair.'

Steel was probably the most fiery footballer of them all, destined to make headline news almost from the moment he first kicked a ball.

Steel was born in Denny in the early twenties and in 1937 he started on the road to fame when he was capped as a schoolboy for Scotland—George Young was in the same team—and attracted scouts by the score.

From then on, no player of his class and talent had a stormier career. He went to Leicester City, but, as he was an under-age youngster, the English club couldn't hold him and he returned to Scotland to play for St. Mirren in 1939. At sixteen he was too young to be signed as a professional. On his seventeenth birthday he joined Greenock Morton. Two years later he went to war in the Royal Corps of Signals and rejoined Morton in December 1946.

From then on, honours—and blazing controversy—filled

his football life. Injury haunted him, too. Yet Steel was a re-
markably cheerful individual. And, unlike some notable footballers, he liked the Press. He took a keen interest in the football reporters' craft and often I spent hours with him talking
about how matches should be described and discussing the
styles of writers. Billy, indeed, became a newspaperman himself—and a good one, for he had a feeling for words and he
expressed himself in print as forcibly as he did on the football field. He is now a newspaper executive in California.

In 1947, however, there were no clouds on Billy Steel's
horizon, Inside six months he had become the 'Golden Boy',
the 'Blond Bombshell' of football.

He made his international début for Scotland in April
of that year at Wembley, his lucky ground, and so dramatic-
ally brilliant was his performance that club cheque-books were
being opened almost before he had unlaced his boots.

A month later Steel had made himself the most-wanted
inside-forward in Britain. He was catapulted into the 'match
of the century'—Great Britain *v.* the Rest of Europe at Hampden. Here was real fame, for at that time Britain was rich in
outstanding forwards. The selectors, however, passed over
Raich Carter, Peter Doherty, Jimmy Hagan, Len Shackleton
and Stan Mortensen. They chose Steel and Wilf Mannion,
another often wayward genius.

A better shop window for Steel, 5 ft. 6 in. of sheer football
talent, could not have been imagined—and Billy, who had
told me he wanted to earn at least £20,000 out of football
before he retired, made the most of it. At that time Morton
were asking a record fee for their star. Steel, who had once
worked in the Denny treasurers' office and had an acute sense
of finance, realised that if he made a hit on football's most
glamorous occasion the offers for him would mount.

He wasn't, I am sure, too happy about the role given to

him by team manager Walter Winterbottom. Steel was to be the grafter of the British line, playing from behind the other forwards, his main job being to push the ball through the middle to centre-forward Tommy Lawton, the rover. Lawton, in turn, had to take Steel's passes and transfer them quickly to Wilf Mannion.

It was an exacting role in such an important match for a lad of Steel's experience. Billy stuck to it manfully, refusing to strike attitudes or attempt any of the solo thrusts for which he was famous, supplying his more exalted colleagues with neat passes.

Then came the thirty-fourth minute. Britain were leading 2—1, but the Rest side had started to hit back. Steel won a tackle, brought the ball cleverly under control and started to dash down the middle. He looked for an unmarked man. But Matthews, Mannion, Lawton and Liddell were all covered. There was only one thing for it—if you were a genius like Steel. He strode on and on. Still the defenders refused to come out. In the Rest goal, brilliant French goalkeeper Da Rui bawled anxiously: *'Regardez Steel.'* No one did. And Steel was twenty yards from goal and he heard Lawton shout: 'Hit it.' Billy did, trying to burst the ball. It was a goal in a million. The ball had flashed, a speed-blurred blob, past the helpless Da Rui—and that goal had added £5,000 to Steel's soaring market value.

Steel had arrived in a big way. In the summer of 1947, after a remarkable auction, Steel was transferred to Derby Countly, then a power in football, for £15,500, a massive sum in those days.

At Derby, Steel blossomed. He revelled in the tough English football. He became even more incisive. His bewildering thrusts were a headache to all opposing defences.

But volatile Billie also became a headache to his club.

Coolly he decided he wanted to live and train in Glasgow —300 miles away from Derby. He was adamant; the club grew exasperated. The troubles of Steel had started.

Derby directors weren't pleased when their flamboyant star set a new style for footballers by calling a full-scale Press conference to explain his point of view. He told us that he had decided he must place his business future before his football career, was going to open a new shop in Glasgow—and he felt he must be on the spot to safeguard his interests.

For a week after week the big row, Steel against Derby County, made headlines. Although he was the hero of every Scottish fan and an automatic choice for the international team, he refused Derby's re-signing offers for five months. Like James and other obstinate Scottish players, he wouldn't budge if he felt he were in the right.

Restlessness marked Steel's nature; always he craved for something new.

Again he got his wish. In 1950 George Anderson, brilliant football impresario behind Dundee, stepped in.

All Scotland rejoiced when Dundee paid a fabulous sum, believed to be £23,000, to bring Steel back from England.

It was a brilliant stroke by the prince of showmen. When Steel made his début against Aberdeen at Dens Park the attendance soared to more than 30,000. Dundee won 2—0 and Steel scored one of the goals. And Dundee were on the way to the most glamorous period in their history.

Steel revolutionised the team. The style was fashioned around him. They won the League Cup twice and went to the final of the Scottish Cup. And a new fashion was set for provincial Scotland. Dundee travelled first-class, lived first-class—and thought first-class.

And everywhere Dundee went the crowds turned up—to watch the colourful Steel. He was worth watching. In these

C

early 'fifties Steel brought adventure back to Scottish soccer. His speed off the mark, his fiery dash, his thundering shot, his facility for appearing in the open space—these wonderful qualities made him the darling of the Dens Park fans.

But under the surface there were rumblings. There were too many angry words between Steel and his team-mates. The Dundee players appreciated their colleague's brilliance—but not his tongue-lashings. And it was inevitable that Steel and George Anderson should clash. Both men liked their own way; both were just too big for a Scottish provincial club.

And suddenly the honeymoon was over.

The first signs of the crack came as they had come at Derby. Steel had a genuine affection for Glasgow and he decided he wanted to live and work in the city, visiting Dundee only for matches and special training sessions. Reluctantly, Dundee agreed to Steel's wishes and he became a journalist with a national paper.

The situation couldn't last. Relations between Steel and Anderson became increasingly strained. Several times Steel was asked to go through to Dens for special training. Always he refused.

Typically, Steel didn't tell Dundee the real reason he didn't want to train at Dens. He had an ankle so badly damaged that he was scared to let the trainer see it. It had been permanently damaged by years of ruthless tackling and it swelled like a balloon after every match and forced Steel to stay in bed all day on Sundays.

Everyone would have sympathised had he told the truth about his injury. But he refused to tender an alibi as long a he himself was prepared to play.

Steel had a fetish about fitness. I saw him in his great days at training give displays of handsprings and somersaults which would have made him a hit in a circus—an example of the agility that made him such a notable footballer.

For a man who could walk the breadth of a football pitch on his hands the thought that one of his limbs was imperfect brought deep depression. He hated the idea that he was no longer physically perfect, even though no one else knew it.

The sands were running out for Steel. He couldn't train as hard as he wanted to, became overweight, slightly podgy— and it was hell for him to listen to criticism, for he would have trained all day had he been fit.

Again Steel made headlines. He broke with Dundee when still apparently at the height of his powers. He was still only in his early thirties, he had won thirty-two caps for Scotland, he was still an international contender, still a magic name and still among the biggest crowd-pullers in football.

He was dropped by Dundee in November 1953. Steel found that hard to forgive, though he was still keeping his injury secret.

And in July 1954 he decided to emigrate to America. He played there for a spell and, as you might have expected, his career was stormy.

He had flashed across the football firmament like a meteor, brilliant but transient. Few players made such an impression on the game by sheer genius; few so tragically failed to make the best of their gifts.

For all his exuberance and opportunism, Steel was never a player who resorted to shady practices. He didn't have to. But continual fouling and crude efforts to stop him took their toll.

Like all great players, he was too often a marked man. As he was in Vienna in May 1951, when 65,000 Austrians bayed for blood in the roughest play in which Scotland ever took part.

There was bad blood between Austria and Scotland and the international became a kicking match. Steel went for a high ball, an Austrian player came from behind him to play the ball, they collided—and, to his consternation, Billy was ordered off.

It was no laughing matter, but Billy always smiled when he recounted what happened after that. 'During my lone and long walk to the pavilion,' he said, 'a woman in the crowd broke through the police cordon, dashed up to me and swung her umbrella. It missed by a fraction.

'Then came the greatest humiliation. I was only four yards from the dressing-room door. The crowd was screaming hysterically. A policeman opened the door. Thankfully I ran in. And then I got a fearful kick in the pants.

'I turned in a flash and saw the kicker was a bloke in Tyrolean outfit, feathered hat, short pants, blouse and jacket. He was about six feet tall, but I was hopping mad and I squared up to him. Luckily for me that was as far as I got. Five policemen grabbed me, heaved me into the dressing-room and locked the door.'

'Steely'—his nickname and where could you find a better? —was up before the S.F.A. Referee Committee when the Scottish party returned home. But several members of the committee had seen the incident in Vienna and Billy was rightly admonished.

That was what I liked about Billy—his sense of humour. He may have been a £23,000 headache to his club—but he was certainly worth the money Dundee paid for him.

What would he be worth today?

Put him in the same bracket as Denis Law.

Like Law, Steel, though he would have made a sturdy soldier of football fortune anywhere in the world, was deeply patriotic. His great ambition was to play football for Scotland. He never played on a losing Scottish side at Wembley.

I wish we had a Billy Steel in the Scotland team now.

He had faults—who hasn't?—but if ever there was a master of modern football Billy Steel is the name.

4

The Gay Gordon

THERE was no more dignified manager in football than Mr.
William McCartney of Hibernian. His voice was rich and
deep, he was always handsomely tailored and he invariably
wore a flower in his buttonhole. His composure, even in moments of crisis, was admirable.

So his friends could hardly believe their eyes that April
night of 1941 when they saw Mr. McCartney running—yes,
actually running.

It was the end of a friendly match between a Hibernian-
Hearts select and a local junior combination to mark the open-
ing of Beechwood Park, the new ground of the Dundee Lochee
Harp.

And the reason the usually calm Mr. McCartney rushed was
a slim, dark, good-looking youngster who had been playing
centre-forward for the Dundee junior select. He had been in
fascinating form and had scored three times against his immediate opponent—none other than Bobby Baxter, Scottish
international centre-half.

Mr. McCartney, a shrewd judge of a player, knew he had
to work fast. He realised the youngster had also intrigued
Hearts officials. Characteristically he decided he would be first
to talk to the young centre-forward.

His luck was in. He beat his rivals for the signature of the

young player—and there was no wonder he said, long afterwards: 'It was worth the rush.'

For the player was Gordon Smith.

And if ever there was a master of football artistry he was
Gordon Smith.

I am not going to say Smith was the greatest winger of all
time. Indeed, I must repeat here that the players I have chosen
in my selection of great masters of Scottish football are not
necessarily the best players in their positions. The fascination
of football lies in the chasms between the styles. No one can
say one star did more for the game than another. It's merely a
matter of personal preference which style the enthusiast
maintains is best.

Even today you can always start an argument by asking if
Gordon Smith was better than Willie Waddell.

Well, there is no doubt in my mind that Waddell was probably the most paying winger of all time. There was glamour
and colour and excitement every time he was on the ball. You
could almost hear the thunder of his studs as he pelted on and
your pulse raced as he swept powerfully towards goal.

The play of Gordon Smith, on the other hand, was always
nicely muted. You felt when watching him that he had never
any need to stamp, as it were, on the loud pedal, to rampage
down the wing. Musicians have talked about his elegant *con
brio* and even those football enthusiasts who prefer the full-
blooded fray to the coldly scientific battle of wits wouldn't
have wanted Smith to race like a sprinter or rely on power.

Not that Smith wasn't fast. He was—and few had his gift
of ball control and he could shoot accurately and venomously.

Somehow, however, this most graceful of wingers made us
feel that style was all. He was poetry in motion—without, as is
the case with so many players, the slightest trace of McGona-
gall creeping in—and his rippling rhythm brought a glimpse

of true art to a game which is all too often a shoddy exercise by players who are not even skilled journeymen.

Not that Waddell wasn't skilful. He was, indeed, the winger who best combined skill and power.

But you can no more compare Smith and Waddell than you can compare a rhapsody by Brahms to a Wagnerian overture. Both, of course, had star quality—colour, imagination, dedication and inborn talent. Waddell, though, liked to pull out all the stops, whereas Smith appeared to be conserving his energy, playing well within himself and becoming world class by sheer elegance. While Waddell discarded the mute and let go with the vivacious trumpet blast of a Louis Armstrong, Smith, like Maurice Winnick, played the sweetest music this side of heaven.

I'm sure, too, the young fans of today will want to know if Smith were better than Willie Henderson. Again, there is a world of difference in the styles. For instance, when Henderson runs down the wing he spurts along like an Olympics ace; when he decides to baffle opponents he pulls one trick after another like a conjuror producing rabbits from a hat. Smith was never like that.

How did he achieve success, the rather grave, modest man who never really found in a Scotland team the success he achieved when playing for his first love, Hibernian?

Gordon Smith was the third son of a Montrose grocer and he was keen on the game almost from the time he could walk. His grace and style were noted early in his career and, as a youngster in Montrose, Gordon was twice capped in schoolboy internationals. In those days he was a centre-forward and that was the position he occupied with a Kirriemuir juvenile side.

It was while he was with Kirriemuir that he began to consider whether he might be a success in football. One day he walked to the top of a hill, from where you can see the 'Window of Thrums', made famous by J. M. Barrie, the Kirriemuir boy whose *Peter Pan* has earned undying fame.

Outside the cricket pavilion a gardener was weeding. Gordon, still in short pants, stopped to chat to him. And he learned from the gardener how Barrie had returned, rich and famous, to present the pavilion to his village.

The small Gordon was deeply impressed by the story of Barrie. He went to the local library and obtained books about the famous writer and every night he read a little of that success story and determined that he, too, would earn fame.

He worked hard at football, studying the methods of the stars and learning how to master the ball. Soon junior clubs were angling for his signature. Dundee North End were the lucky club. And then on to Hibernian went Smith.

It was there his future was really decided. He was switched to outside-right.

And it was then he decided that he would try to make his name as a football artist.

Not that Smith, a realist as well as a highly imaginative thinker, thought for a moment that art is all in football. He told me once:

'You can argue for hours, without reaching a conclusion favourable to all, about whether football is an art or a sport. It is probably a combination of both.

'Some of the taller brows feel that what really matters in the end is the style of the performance but professional football is also a business and the average fan in Scotland wants, first and foremost, to see his team win. Besides skill, the will to win must be firmly implanted into the mind of any aspiring professional footballer.

'But while realising that football in Scotland is a mixture of so many different methods I must say that I prefer the graceful approach and I believe that pure skill and craftsmanship will always triumph over more enthusiastic, brawny tactics.'

And there was no one ever more graceful than Gordon Smith.

Grace? Was that his real secret? No. Deep thought—that is what made Smith stand out.

Like all real footballers he was a fine player without the ball. Few wingers, apart from Stanley Matthews, were as closely marked as Smith. Yet few were able to give themselves so much room in which to receive and control the ball—initially. To get the ball Smith often went back into his own half—or across the field. And when he had possession there were few defenders who could rob him. He had the footwork of a champion lightweight boxer; his crosses were perfection; he was complete master of the ball.

That is the hallmark of the truly great player.

But to spend as long at the top as Smith did you need more than ball control.

A smile from the goddess fame?

Certainly fame is a fickle goddess, especially in sport, and too many of those she has endowed with rare talent have been expelled from the deity with contemptuous suddenness. Or so it seems at first glance. Especially Scots.

But when you examine the cases of the cast-out stars you usually discover that the goddess fame is not so much fickle as stern and that the favourites she has scorned have squandered her gifts.

So many have fallen from grace—the boxer who prefers the *dolce vita* to the rigours of heart-straining roadwork, the footballer who saps his skill by lush living.

The tragedy is that the stars who crash are sometimes those blessed with the greatest natural talent.

But—and maybe this is the curse on Scotland's sportsmen —they take their ability for granted, consider themselves favourites on whom the goddess will always smile and believe they will reign for ever.

They don't, of course. They dissipate their gifts.

When you think of Gordon Smith, however, you realise there is nothing to compare with a fabulous gift of rare talent plus awesome dedication, sincere gratitude for the gifts so liberally granted and a fierce determination to make the best use of it.

It is when you consider Gordon Smith that you know why the goddess Fame gave such short shrift to others who took her donations—and squandered them.

For Smith was a humble footballer, quiet and reserved and shy—which was why some thought he was arrogant and chilly. He wasn't.

He was ever grateful for the talent that was given him. He was determined to make the best of it. Which was why when approaching the age of forty he was still as supple as a stripling, as graceful as a ballet dancer, as fit as a Sherpa of Everest.

No wonder he was beloved of the goddess Fame. Gordon Smith used her gifts exactly as she intended—and there can be no more shining example to the up-and-coming footballer than Smith, the perfect model to advertise all that is best in the game.

But how, cries the young man who wants to be a new Gordon Smith, can one ever achieve the skill of the superman of soccer? True, that may be impossible; there may never again be a winger as entrancing as Smith. But the young player can find inspiration in the story of Smith—and he must succeed if he follows and the methods and way of football life laid down by the maestro.

Smith lived for football. As he once told me: 'Football is an obsession with me and I play it for the real joy of the game itself.'

Few players, though, worked as hard as Smith and few had his burning ambition to reach the top—and stay there.

When you recall that Smith signed for Hibernian in 1941 and did not retire—when he was still pretty near the top—until the middle 1960's you probably believe Gordon had a magic potion.

I once asked him just that. Smith smiled at the thought. 'Magic? No.' A pause. 'No, there's nothing magic about my methods. I live for football, give it everything.'

Some would have thought Gordon Smith was exaggerating somewhat when he said that. For at that time he was—as he is today—a prosperous businessman, a fine golfer, a music enthusiast. But golf, music and business, he insisted, were his hobbies. Football was still there, in 1963, his business and his life.

That you would have believed if, on a bleak winter's morning, you had seen a stranger on the shore at North Berwick, a lonely figure practising football, keeping fit on a bare beach swept by sleet and a biting wind. The stranger was Smith, at thirty-eight years of age, training, training, training to keep himself in the perfect trim required by a top-flight professional footballer of this modern era in which stamina and power have never been more essential—and Smith essentially an artist.

Early in his career, though, Gordon Smith realised that if he were to play football well he would have to make sacrifices.

For instance, on smoking: 'When I was fourteen it was made obvious to me by my teacher, Mr. James Edward, of

Montrose South Esk School, that smoking was a bad thing for footballers. So for me it was out.

'No. I've never smoked. Well, once or twice when I was about eight—and I was violently sick.'

But these are Smith's personal views on smoking. He never tried to ram his ideas down anyone else's throat. Perhaps he should have. For his live-and-let-live attitude sometimes annoyed his colleagues, brasher, more extrovert, who couldn't understand his reserve.

Again on smoking: 'It's not for me to preach to others. I have known heavy smokers among my colleagues and they were good players.

'Well, it could have been that I might have smoked and gone on playing as long as I have. But I don't know and I don't care. All I know is that I felt smoking was bad for me as a footballer and I just didn't adopt the habit.'

There was another reason Smith was at the top as a professional footballer for a quarter of a century: his attitude to food.

I have toured many times with Scotland—but never have I known anyone like Gordon Smith to refrain from sampling the delicacies of foreign cities.

He never ate between meals, never touched white sugar or white bread. At eight he had a light breakfast—two apples, a glass of milk and perhaps an orange. And the fruit had to be fresh. Smith never ate out of tins.

He had at least five hours between meals. At two o'clock he had a steak and at 7.30 he had meat again—or fish. He didn't eat or drink again before going to bed.

A faddist? Not at all. Indeed, Smith's views on eating—and they haven't changed much since he retired from football—should be studied by all who want to be fit and well as the years catch up.

He never touched fried food. 'On the odd occasion,' he said, 'I have been persuaded to take chips. It may be imagination—but I haven't felt the same afterwards.'

Travel abroad made things difficult for Smith. He flew practically all over the world to play football. In 1945 he was in the Scotland side which met the British Forces' team in Germany.

Since that year he was abroad almost every season for Scotland, eighteen years for Hibs, two years for Hearts and then more and more flights to the Continent with Dundee.

Some of these travels were troublesome. His worst time was with Dundee in Iceland in 1961. He didn't like the food —unusual fish dishes.

He liked America, however. 'Although you might think the temptations would be great to overeat in the States,' he told me, 'I found it suited me fine. The Americans go in for fresh fruit and salads and that's just what I like.'

What about drink? Smith says quietly—and he is still a quiet man, Smith, sure of his own opinions but never trying to be dogmatic, to insist that he alone is right in his theories: 'I took the odd spot, special occasions and things like that. Oh, yes, I took a drink when I was playing, but I didn't believe in drinking. Always I asked myself: Will it do my football any harm? If I thought that it would, then it was out.

'It's what you think that matters and the way you obey the results of your thinking.'

That, then, was the difference between Smith and so many other great Scottish players who disappeared long before they had reached their prime.

He never let fame go to his head. He was an artist—with an athlete's dedication.

He is out of football now. More's the pity. Few knew more

about tactics than Smith. But I don't think he'll come back. He is content in his business.

I'm content that I saw him, knew him.

Not only was Gordon Smith a master of football, a pleasant travelling companion . . . he is an inspiration to youth.

5

Prince of Goalkeepers

IN NO other position in a football eleven has the truth been proved so consistently of Abraham Lincoln's assertion that 'it is better to adhere to the old and tried than to the new and untried'. In no other position have there been as many players who grew old and grey in the service of their clubs as goalkeepers. They broke the hearts of reserves who could never oust them, the great keepers like Jerry Dawson, Jimmy Brown, Bartram, Sagar, Sidlow, Ditchburn, Johnstone, McClory, Ronnie Simpson.

For it is one position in which age is never a real handicap; indeed, it is only from experience that a goalkeeper can acquire the mathematical, meteorological and psychological learning that is essential to his job. The good keeper must be able to bisect angles in order to perplex an eager forward or to deflect rising balls over the bar. He must sense what effect wind or rain may have on a corner kick or a high cross. And he must be something of a psychologist to anticipate the probable direction of a shot. Besides, of course, having some of the qualities of an acrobat, the courage of a lion and the eye of a hawk—the gifts to youth which seem never to depart from ageing goalies.

And yet . . . and yet . . . the goalkeeper I nominate as prince of his trade was only twenty-two when he died, hardly in the flush of manhood. But even at that tender age, as far as foot-

Alex James

Jim Baxter

Billy Steel

Patsy Gallacher—the Matthews look?

John Thomson, prince of goalkeepers, is far right in the back row of this great old Celtic team, in which the players are: *from left to right—back row*, Cook, McGonagle, Thomson; *middle row*, Geatons, Scarf, Wilson, Alec Thomson; *front row*, McGrory, Napier, McStay, and Bertie Thomson

Opposite, Denis Law

Alan Morton

Jimmy Mason

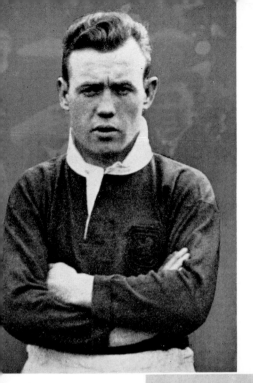

Hughie Gallacher

George Young

Gordon
Smith

ballers go, he had become a legend. For he was John Thomson, Scotland's most loved player.

The name is still revered in Scotland. To thousands of Celtic supporters who weren't born when Thomson died he is still the best goalkeeper who ever played. It is true his tragic death made him a hero for whom ballads were written, a footballer who will never be forgotten. But we must realise that when he played he was hailed as a genius, even though he was so young. He magnetised the fans; he was an idol. There was a story—and it was true—that when he was at a children's party in a house in Fife a small ball was produced and, with the grown-ups next door preparing supper, the fun grew fast and furious. Too furious . . . A lad kicked the ball straight at the oil lamp on the table. Disaster seemed certain—until a slim boy reacted with the speed which was to make him famous years afterwards. He hurled himself through the air with panther's grace and caught the ball just as tragedy seemed imminent. You could believe it of John Thomson.

I saw him through boy's eyes and every time I saw him I knew I was watching a superb goalkeeper who had every gift.

He was, I think, the first of a new breed of goalkeeper. Until Thomson arrived on the scene goalkeepers in Scotland tended to be sober, dignified fellows. They dressed sombrely and the cloth cap they affected gave them the appearance of foremen, who, as all the world knows, are not noted for flamboyance.

Then there was the Scottish environment of that age. There was little time for drama or histrionics. The showy character was disliked and well might retire the goalkeeper of whom it was said contemptuously: 'Ach, he mak's the easy yins look hard.' The keeper who tried to invest his game with colour was looked on with deep-rooted suspicion and had as much chance of making a successful career in Scotland in those days

D

as a bank clerk who went to work in sports jacket and flannels.

But Thomson was different. Perhaps it was his essential niceness; perhaps it was his youthful eagerness. More likely, it was because, despite his agility, his new ideas, his spectacular leaps, everyone realised no more reliable goalkeeper could have been found anywhere in the world.

He was thoughtful, defiant, brave, inspiring tremendous confidence in the men in front of him, always watching play, combining rare, natural talent with a mathematical precision that took so many of the risks out of his often hazardous art.

Alas, in the end he sacrificed that precision for blind, instinctive, courageous play.

John Thomson was a knight in an old-fashioned roll-necked pullover, one of the game's true romantics, the prince in the fairy-tale.

There was nothing romantic, however, about his early days. John Thomson was born in Kirkcaldy, the son of a miner. He, too, went into the pits when he was barely fourteen, but he knew that his future lay in football.

He could have played anywhere with distinction and those who saw him at practice declared he was a born ball-worker. He loved football and every spare minute was spent with a ball.

Although he could have chosen his position, he had really no wish to play anywhere except in goal. That was where he played with Wellesley, a junior club, and his stylish, mature displays made him a local hero. Perhaps even at this early stage John knew that his future lay with Celtic, for the shirts of Wellesley were green and white, just like those of the mighty Parkhead men.

And yet it was by accident that he joined Celtic in 1926 when he was only seventeen.

A Celtic scout went to Fife to watch a goalkeeper who was

playing for Dunbeath and of whom he had heard glowing reports.

What became of that lad we never found out—for the Celtic scout couldn't keep his eyes off the goalkeeper in the opposite goal.

That keeper was John Thomson, of Wellesley, and at once the scout's experienced eye told him that he had discovered a goalkeeper who had future internationalist stamped on all his play. The thin boy had a veteran's coolness, uncanny anticipation, a sure clutch and an acrobat's agility. Certainly he seemed to be inspired that day he was first seen by a Parkhead scout, and he even saved a penalty.

No time was wasted by the scout. He interviewed John and persuaded him to sign for Celtic. It is said the scout produced the form and held it against a telegraph pole for support as Thomson put his name to it. He was paid the usual signing-on fee of £10.

Thomson's meteoric career had begun.

But there was no blaze of glory for John Thomson at the start.

Old Celtic players still recall the arrival of John Thomson in Glasgow—a shy, fresh-faced boy in a long blue coat and a huge cap. But at once he became a favourite with the players, so friendly was his manner, so eager was he to learn his craft.

He played steadily enough in the Celtic reserve side. But when he was promoted to the first team, some of the officials wondered if they had made a mistake in signing him. For John Thomson lost a goal which would have made the most ham-handed junior blush.

It was in 1927 that John played his first game for Celtic—against Dundee in a League fixture at Dens Park.

Early in the game, wee Willie Cook, the famous Dundee

outside-left, put a high ball over goal. It didn't look dangerous and the slim laddie in the Celtic goal stretched his arms easily and casually to field it. But there was no firm slap of hands on ball. John let it slip and he couldn't recover in time and the ball slithered into the net and it was a goalie's nightmare. John hung his head in shame.

But he had learned a vital lesson early—and never again did he go for a ball half-heartedly. Even for 'keepers' he was down or up, giving his full concentration, his full power to fielding the ball.

Celtic won the game 2—1 and John was mildly ticked off for losing a silly goal—but he stayed in the first eleven—and became the foremost goalkeeper of his day.

John Thomson would have been a great goalkeeper in any age because of his hands and his eye. His hands were those of a surgeon's, fine but powerful. He made the crowd gasp when he stopped powerful shots and held the ball securely when lesser keepers would have been glad merely to have stopped it.

He had an athlete's eye and he was brilliant at nearly every other ball game, especially golf.

But John had more than that.

His true greatness lay in the way he could find extra power to change course and find fresh drive in mid-air. Today he would probably have been nicknamed Batman.

He has been compared with the great Negro athlete Jesse Owens, for he had a physical peculiarity equivalent to the hitch-kick Owens gave half-way through his long jump when competing at the Berlian Olympiad which enabled him to put up a world record.

When John was in the air he could give himself an additional thrust and so turn himself in another direction or gain him additional inches in his spring. I have gazed, awed, as he revealed his magic, twisting in mid-air to hurl himself the other way when deceived by a shot.

So John Thomson, a pleasant-faced boy with a hair style which would now be known as a 'long crew-cut', became Scotland's goalkeeper.

He stood unrivalled. There was no one in his class and football fans of clubs other than Celtic say to this day there never has, or ever will be, a goalkeeper of the style, daring and brilliance of John Thomson.

He received eight Scottish caps. If he had lived he would have received countless more. The boy from Fife had arrived.

He didn't change, though. Despite the adulation he received, he was still the shy country boy, always ready to take a word of advice, always willing to help a youngster coming up. He was the hero of Scotland but he still continued to practise all day for he loved the game.

To what heights Thomson would have risen no one can tell, for he died before he had reached his full stature as a goalkeeper, although the skill he had attained has never been equalled.

It was a bright September afternoon of 1931 when John Thomson made his last save—the 5th of September, the most sorrowful day in the history of Scottish football.

There was no hint of tragedy, however, as 80,000 spectators rolled gaily into Ibrox for the first meeting of the season between Rangers and Celtic. The sunny afternoon had put everyone in high spirits.

In the Celtic dressing-room the players chaffed John as he put in his customary last-minute practice, throwing the ball in the air and catching it, to test his grip and get his eye in. Thomson never left anything to chance.

When the game started Rangers went into the attack. Playing against Celtic for the first time was the able young Rangers centre-forward Sam English. In the opening raid he missed narrowly with a good header. Always a fine sportsman, always keen to see newcomers do well, John grinned at his opponent and said: 'Hard lines.'

But the first half had been rather dull.

Then came the tragic second period.

Five minutes had gone. The ball broke clear towards the Celtic goal. Sam English saw his chance. He was away on his own, in hot pursuit of the ball. Only Thomson stood between him and a goal.

The Celtic goalkeeper realised the danger. Only for a split second did he hesitate. In fact, it was part of his policy not to leave his charge if he could possibly avoid it and only the previous week he had written an instructional article in a Sunday newspaper with these very words in it: 'Never leave your goal unless in a great emergency.'

Certainly this time the emergency was great. Thomson knew there was no alternative if a goal was to be prevented.

He ran out and he dived like a scrum-half right at English's feet and the centre-forward could do nothing about it, for his boot was already lifted to shoot and the speed of Thomson's leap took him unawares.

John Thomson's head hit the centre-forward's knee as he dived at his feet. English rose, limping. Thomson lay still. And the ball, deflected, rolled slowly past the empty net. A certain goal had been averted.

But at what a cost.

Thomson didn't move. Anxiously the other players gathered round him. It was obvious the injury was serious and a stretcher was called for.

Behind the goal, the crowd did not understand the extent

of the goalkeeper's injury and they shouted and cheered, exalting in a knock to an opponent.

Not until the worried Davie Meiklejohn, the famous Ranger, moved to the back of the goal to signal to the rowdy Ibrox fans that Thomson was badly hurt did they stop their row.

To their credit, the noisy supporters later wrote a letter to a daily newspaper to apologise for their conduct and to say: 'It has proved a lesson to us.'

Meanwhile, John Thomson had been taken on the stretcher to the pavilion. Once he rose and looked towards his goal. Then he slumped back.

In the pavilion he was examined by Dr. Kivlichan, himself a former Celtic and Rangers player, and Dr. Gillespie, and then taken to the Victoria Infirmary in Glasgow.

His injury was diagnosed as compressed fracture of the skull. His father and mother were brought post-haste from Cardenden, Fife, but they only saw John alive for a few minutes. He died five hours after the match, without regaining consciousness.

All Scotland mourned. The fans were stunned. The game had been robbed of one of its most beloved players. For John Thomson was a man without an enemy, as popular with supporters of other clubs as he was with the fans of Celtic, hero-worshipped by every small boy in Scotland, a sportsman without a blemish, the model athlete.

Press, clergy and officials paid him high tributes. One minister said: 'John Thoson died accomplishing an act of superb and uncalculating gallantry. His courage was supreme, his loyalty unfaltering.'

The scenes at his funeral have never been paralleled in Scottish sporting history. Thirty thousand people jammed the road between his home in Cardenden and the cemetery less than a mile away to which he was borne by his fellow players. And 20,000 others stood silently at a Glasgow station to see his mourners leave that city by special trains.

Such was the affection for the goalkeeper that many others had left by foot, determined to be at the funeral, scores of miles away. No one could calculate how many wreaths were sent to the graveside. A railway wagon was packed with floral tributes.

Pipe and silver bands, with muffled drums, headed the funeral procession, in which footballers of many eras were represented, marching silently side by side.

It was an impressive tribute to the laddie who had become the idol of thousands.

There was sympathy, too, for Sam English, who had no chance whatever of avoiding the accident, and at the inquiry afterwards the sheriff said to the jury: 'You are satisfied from the evidence that the affair was accidental and you return a verdict as follows:

'That the deceased, while engaged in his employment as a professional footballer with Celtic Football Club and acting as goalkeeper in a football match with Rangers at Ibrox Park, Glasgow, in the course of the match sustained injuries to his head by accidentally coming in contact with the body of Samuel English, playing centre-forward for Rangers, in an attempt to save a goal by diving towards Samuel English while in the act of kicking the ball and received a fracture of the skull from which he died in the Victoria Infirmary.'

As was said at the time: 'While engaged in his employment . . . in an attempt to save a goal'—that was the epitaph the unassuming John Thomson would have liked best himself.

He has been dead these many years, but his memory lives on, undimmed.

He brought romance to thousands, at a time when there was little that glittered in Scottish life.

Truly, he made goalkeeping an art.

6

The Moody Genius

THE great Scottish footballers have never been strong, silent men. Most of them were wee wisps with fiery tempers and whiplash tongues. Even today Scottish players are great talkers, and crowds abroad, unaccustomed to running commentaries on the field of play, grow restive as they are assailed by a Doric cacophony of yelps, bawls, complaints, snarls, advice, encouragement, condemnation and appeal.

And it is as well that foreign players seldom understand what their Scottish opponents are saying to them; otherwise, there would be mayhem. For nothing can be crueller than a venomous insult about one's parentage, lack of courage, immoral way of life or looks delivered in rich Scottish accent.

No one in football history, however, had a tongue like Hughie Gallacher, moody genius, man of mystery, probably the greatest centre-forward of all time. Alex James was a natural chatterbox; Billy Steel's burning determination to win too often made him lash colleagues. But Hughie had the cheekiest tongue of them all—and he used it on an opponent instead of the boot.

He was never a dirty player. How could he be? He had neither height nor weight to make power his ally. And those old-timers who saw Gallacher's scarred, hacked legs after a match agreed that if Hughie hadn't talked he would have burst out of sheer frustration.

Gallacher was the enigma of football, however, a many-sided character, his own worst enemy, often regretting rash outbursts, turning enemies into friends with startling kind-nesses.

There was, for instance, the experience of Alex Hastings, once Sunderland and Scotland wing-half. 'I can never forget the first time I played against Hughie Gallacher,' Alex said. 'I was just eighteen and starting with Sunderland. Hughie was with Chelsea and this was the first time he had played in the north-east since he left Newcastle. So Roker Park was packed. Hughie was still an idol in the north-east. Everyone wanted to see him.

'I was nervous, I can tell you. For Gallacher was at inside-right and I was at left-half. And I never hated anyone so much. You might have thought a great player like Hughie would have had some thought for a rookie like myself and a fellow Scot. Not a bit of it. From the kick-off he was snarling at me. He offered to stay the week-end in Sunderland and give me lessons on how to kick a ball. Then he remarked it was a shame my parents should allow a big sapsy like me to leave home. And on and on he pattered.

'I was seething, very upset. But I didn't let him see I was worried. And when he realised he wasn't riling me—or didn't appear to be—he gave it up and concentrated on playing. And how he could play.

'Anyhow, at the end of the game I was still bitterly angry. And then Gallacher came into the dressing-room and held out his hand. He smiled: "Good luck to you, son. You can take it. I'm sorry I needled you. But you know me. I just canna' help it." '

And Hughie couldn't. It was his way. His bark was always worse than his bite and, despite all his moodiness, he was essentially a fair man.

There was the time when the directors of his club, New-castle United, called him in to ask for guidance. It was during the late 1920's, the golden era of football, and United were looking for a centre-half. Nothing but the best would do for the club which was to become known as 'The Bank of England' team. Money was no object and the board decided that the right man to name the outstanding centre-half was their own centre-forward, the best in the land, the man who knew the strengths and weaknesses of his immediate opponents.

Hughie was only too willing to help. First he suggested David Meiklejohn, of Rangers, as the best in football.

But the Ibrox club only laughed at Newcastle's offer. So Gallacher suggested the next best, Jack Hill, of Burnley. And the directors gasped.

They thought Gallcher and the big-raw-boned Hill were bitter enemies and certainly there had always been 'needle' when these two clashed.

'Surely you can't want Hill as a club-mate?' Gallacher was asked. Hughie didn't even smile. He said quietly: 'Hill has held me and if he can do that he can master any centre-forward in the country.' Conceited? Not a bit of it. Gallacher knew his worth. He knew Hill's, too. He was a loyal club man and even if Hill had been his deadly foe he would still have re-commended the centre-half if he thought he was the best man for the position.

Hill, of course, was only Gallacher's enemy when they clashed on the football field. He once said: 'Actually, Hughie and I were the best of pals. We had tough clashes, it's true, but there was never bitterness after the game. And when I joined United on his recommendation we were almost in-separable.'

No player, not James, not Law, not Steel, not Young, not Morton, ever received higher praise than Gallacher. You can judge for yourself why he was rated the world's greatest centre-forward from these unsolicited testimonials:

Jimmy Boyd, a noted Scottish player who was in the same Newcastle United side as Gallacher, 'There was never anyone like Hughie. He would have run rings round Hidegkuti and Di Stefano.'

Frank Watt, who was secretary of Newcastle, 'Gallacher was the greatest player, not merely the greatest centre-forward, I have ever known.'

To me, Gallacher was the great master centre-forward. On the field he was perfection. And it is by his play on the field that we must judge a footballer. Gallacher had his faults, his weaknesses; and, like too many superb Scottish athletes, the spotlight of fame was too bright for him.

There was, however, no blemish in his play. He was the centre-forward who had everything: footwork, body swerve, powerful shot, astonishing heading ability. That wasn't all. What made him a footballing genius was his ability to do the unexpected, to turn up in the right spot when it seemed impossible for him to get there. And one of his gifts was a toughness of spirit which enable him to take on the most powerful opponents and, as his admirers said, 'kid the life out of them'.

It was said that Gallacher was tough, truculent and a troublemaker. He was tough. He had to be, for he was only five feet six inches tall and never weighed more than eleven stone in his playing days. He was fearless, too. But the only trouble he ever caused was with his tongue. It is true that he said, when asked if he had a terrible temper: 'Well, I suppose I'm said to be pretty tough but no one is going to try and knit me into wire netting and get away with it—and I'm not going to get kicked up in the air and reply with a saintly smile.'

And Hughie would scowl and look fierce and the interviewer went away convinced the wee Scot would be kicking and hacking like mad in his next game. Nothing was further from the truth. He would jeer and snarl and insult opponents —but never did Gallacher go in for illegal tackling or kicking. He didn't have to. He knew his best reply was to score goals.

Few people ever got close to Gallacher, however. He was, indeed, football's man of mystery and he was often shrouded in Celtic melancholy. His was an ill-starred life, alas, and though he was a man born to fame and adulation his career had moments of mysticism never known before or after in football history.

In 1924–25, for example, Gallacher was chosen to play for Scotland against Wales at Tynecastle. There was drama when an Irish journalist alleged that Hughie wasn't eligible to play for Scotland as he had been born in Belfast. And the reporter produced what he said were extracts from an Irish births registration office, with names and occupations of parents exactly similar and the date of birth also identical.

There was real fuss—until an indignant Mrs. Gallacher brought out her son Hughie's certificate, signed and stamped at a parish adjoining Bellshill, near Glasgow. And yet another Gallacher canard had been blown sky-high.

There was another Irish incident. Gallacher had played superbly against the Irish League and partisan home fans who were angry because he had humbled their defence threatened him.

Setting out to visit friends in Belfast after the match, Hughie was warned to be careful. He grinned—until a bullet splattered on a nearby wall. Whether it was a real attempt on his life or a grim practical joke will never be known.

Consider, too, Gallacher's foreboding in his greatest match of all—the Wembley Wizards game at Wembley, which Scotland won 5—1.

Hughie played for ninety minutes with a gremlin over his shoulder. He knew something was wrong; he had a premonition. It was nothing to do with his play for he was brilliant. But he worried. And soon after the match ended he was informed that his sister-in-law had died before he left Scotland for the international. The news had been kept from him deliberately. Still, he had that presentiment.

It is said of many players: 'He is worth his weight in gold'. That was really true of Gallacher; indeed, on the scales he would have been worth two and a half times his weight in gold. He figured in transfer fees totalling £23,000—and 10,000 sovereigns equals around eleven stone, Hughie's weight. If he had been playing today his fees would have been ten times the amounts clubs paid for him in the 1920's.

As a boy, Hughie was keen enough on football and his father once told me: 'I couldn't keep Hughie in boots when he was a laddie. I even bought him a pair of wooden clogs but he split them playing football in the park.' His main ambition, however, was to be a boxer. He had been born near Bellshill in 1903 and he felt the ring could be his career because two great Scottish champions, Tommy Milligan and Johnny Brown, had been in his school in Hamilton. This ambition, as Hughie confessed, was 'soon knocked out of me—the hard way'. And when he became friendly with Alex James he decided to fall in with his pal's plans and become a footballer. Soon the two lads became the terror of all local defences. Their origin was not uncommon in their part of Scotland—at that time bleak, depressing, a cold, hard countryside around Bellshill. Their only amusement was playing with a tanner ba', that little elusive rubber sphere, as an old-time sports-writer graphically described it, which produced so many superlative artists. The dexterity of Gallacher and James was characteristic of that early background, the matches played in streets and waste ground, and they learned arts of football to counter-balance their lack of inches, for James was hardly as tall as his wee friend.

They graduated to organised football and soon he had the great privilege of carrying the kit hamper of Bellshill Athletic, the local junior team, on Saturdays.

Within two months of leaving school, Hughie Gallacher was picked for Scotland's junior eleven against Ireland and soon he decided to leave his job in the pits, get away from the shadows of grim bings and concentrate on football.

Queen of the South fancied his play and when they made him an offer of £4 a week Hughie quickly accepted.

Almost at once the bad luck that was to haunt him ever afterwards struck. He was stricken by pneumonia and he thought his football career was finished. He shook off the mood of despondency, however, and the determination which was to characterise his play in later years pulled him through.

At this time he had a friend in need in Jock Ewart, Scotland and Airdrieonians goalkeeper. Not only was Jock a brilliant footballer, he was the greatest character of his generation. He was the son of a miner but he could have had a career on the stage. He spoke fluent French and had a passable knowledge of Russian and German. He played the piano, the flute, the violin. He recognised Gallacher's talent and tried to instill confidence in a lad who was becoming withdrawn, worried and unsure of his ability. He succeeded and Gallacher was signed by Airdrie.

In the office of a local undertaker, incidentally!

There was never anything commonplace about Gallacher in football.

Today Gallacher would have been playing in the first team of any senior club within weeks. But away back in the 'twen-

ties no one rocketed to the stars. In those days, when Scottish
football was at its supreme best, Gallacher, even the great
Hughie with all his skill, had to serve a two-year apprenticeship with the Broomfield reserves.

His rare talent earned him what, away back, was rapid pro-
motion and he began to play in the most brilliant side ever
fielded by Airdrie—a side to bring a gleam to the eyes of all
who saw it, a side which won the Scottish Cup in 1923–4. The
names will never be forgotten in Lanarkshire: Ewart; Dick,
McQueen; Preston, McDougall and Bennie; Reid, Russell,
Gallacher, McPhail and Somerville.

And here is another tribute to Gallacher, from Bob Mc-
Phail, who became famous with Rangers: 'It wasn't until I
left Airdrie and saw them play one day that I fully realised
just how much work Hughie Gallacher put into his game.
Playing alongside him, I didn't appreciate what he did. Watching him from the stand, I could hardly believe it. He seemed
to be everywhere, positioning himself for a pass, chasing for
the ball, challenging an opponent double his size.

'He never spared himself, always giving everything he had.
I never saw a player who gave so much for his side.' So it was
no surprise when Hughie received his first full cap—a twenty-
first birthday present. The game was against Ireland at Celtic
Park and Scotland won 2—0.

Then came the international which made Gallacher a hero
and caused many rich English clubs to begin investigating the
leader with the magic goal-scoring touch. It was against Wales
at Tynecastle in 1924–5 and in it Hughie scored his first international goals—and one of them was his greatest.

In the second half the pitch was churned to a quagmire.
Gallacher, on the centre-line, took the heavy, sodden ball. As
he had scored his first goal by pretending to pass, then darting
on himself, no one expected him to repeat the tactic. Anyhow,

E

there were five Welsh stalwarts between him and the goal, including the imperturbable Welsh centre-half Fred Keenor, of Cardiff City. But even Keenor couldn't stop a genius. That's what Gallacher was. And he did it again.

Another lightning turn—and he was streaking upfield, the ball tied to his boot, and he swerved past Keenor almost contemptuously, and then Moses Russell, a back, stuck out a foot to block his progress and Hughie pushed the ball over his stretching leg and ran round him on his blind side.

And now he was nearing goal, but there was still time for defenders to stop him, and out of the corner of his eye Gallacher glimpsed the other back racing in to tackle and there seemed no way past.

Gallacher stopped dead. The back was surprised. He floundered, mistimed his tackle.

And Gallacher was dashing away again, and now he was within shooting distance and his instinct told him that all defenders had been left behind and only the goalkeeper, Gray, stood between him and the goal of a lifetime.

Gray, gallant, did the only thing possible. He dived frantically at the ball. He went down on Gallacher's right foot. And Gallacher coolly hooked the ball over the keeper and tapped it into the net with his left foot. Gallacher said afterwards: 'As I turned to walk back I saw the Welsh defenders applauding me. I wanted to thank them for that. It was great sportsmanship and it was the proudest moment of my life.'

Now Hughie Gallacher was on the crest of the wave. He was Scotland's centre-forward, the hero of every schoolboy. Great English clubs were intrigued. They flashed chequebooks under the noses of the Airdrie directors. They wanted Gallacher.

The directors merely laughed. They had no intention of parting with their star. And rumours of a transfer so annoyed

the Airdrie fans that they threatened to burn down the stand
if Hughie were sold.

But they didn't reckon with Newcastle. Time and time again
Airdrie refused tempting offers from United for their goal-
scoring machine. United kept on trying. And one night the
English club sent a delegation to Airdrie. The Broomfield
directors didn't even want to see them, but the bold Geordies
gate-crashed the board meeting.

The exasperated Airdrie men listened as the Newcastle officials said: 'Name your price for Gallacher.' Jokingly, the Scots
asked for £6,500—a tremendous sum in those days. But Newcastle didn't hesitate. They paid the money—and Gallacher
was bound for St. James Park.

The ground was packed when Hughie made his first appearance for Newcastle. The huge crowd was agog to see their
expensive new player. United were playing Everton, led by
Dixie Dean, England's outstanding centre-forward. This is
how Gallacher described that moment:

'When I ran out to the field suddenly there was a huge
"Ohhh" of disappointment. The crowd had just noticed how
small I was. They thought I was far too wee.'

Other people had thought so, too. Gallacher had been
strongly recommended to Dundee—but the Dens Park people
thought he wasn't big enough either.

Even his Newcastle colleagues were dubious about their
tiny tot. Centre-half Charles Spencer recalled their feelings:
'Gallacher had been a big name in Scotland,' he said, 'but we
were staggered by his lack of inches. But soon after the match
began I turned and gave my fellow defenders a thumbs-up
signal. We knew a real star had joined us.'

And soon Hughie, who had set up a record by scoring five
goals in succession for the Scottish League against the Irish

League in Belfast, was the idol of tough Tyneside, even more popular than he had been in Airdrie.

Football in England, however, was no bed of roses for Gallacher. He had been roughly treated at home—but that was nothing to the Marciano tactics used against him in the more robust soccer south of the border. Often he was black and blue after a match. His smallness was responsible for much of the unarmed combat employed against him.

It was impossible to compute how many fomentations, how many poultices, were applied to his ankles, calves, thighs, hips, chest and back.

And Jack Harkness, the Wembley Wizards goalkeeper, has told me that in the dressing-room before a match Gallacher would pull down his stocking and look at his legs with a sigh. 'I never saw any forward with as many scars and hacks,' said Jack.

Gallacher was not entirely blameless. He didn't foul, but that tongue of his would have upset a saint—and there were precious few saints in football defences. There is no doubt that Gallacher was more sinned against than most and he was not always given adequate protection by referees, for not only boots but fists and elbows were used to stop him.

Hughie was accused of baiting referees, but he had reason for complaint more often than not. And not all referees were his enemies. Indeed, he became a close friend of one, Bert Fogg. And how this came about is another historic Gallacher story.

In a match against Huddersfield Town, then bitter rivals of Newcastle, Gallacher was the constant target of strong-arm opponents. He was crashed time after time. His temper grew hotter and hotter. When Huddersfield won with a penalty kick, Hughie could restrain himself no longer. He snarled at the referee. The official threatened to report him. 'What's your name?' he asked. Hughie snapped: 'You shouldn't be on the field if you don't know. Anyhow, what's your name?'

'I'm Mr. Fogg,' said the startled referee.

Like a flash Gallacher snorted: 'And you've been in one all afternoon.'

The referee couldn't overlook this impertinence, reported the player and Gallacher was suspended for two months. But later the two men became firm friends.

His suspension over—and it wasn't the only time his tongue had him in trouble—Hughie Gallacher was chosen for the Scottish team to meet England at Wembley in 1928—and every Scot, no matter his age, knows that the Wembley Wizards won a famous victory.

Gallacher was at his peak. He believed strongly in himself. He realised an opposing centre-half would have to be an outstanding player to master him, for, by hours of practice, he had turned natural ability into football genius.

In 1927 he was made Newcastle's captain and he led the team to the First Division championship.

This was hardly a wise choice. Gallacher could never have been an ideal captain and it became obvious to the officials that the constant onslaughts against him weren't helping his temper and the directors gave the captaincy to another player.

This made Hughie furious at the time, but he soon saw the directors were right and he concentrated on his full-time job as centre-forward.

In the early 1930's Newcastle signed another centre-forward, Duncan Hutchinson, from Dundee. Gallacher was switched to inside-right. And again there were amazing rumours about Hughie—that he was angry, that he wanted to leave United, that he preferred to play centre-forward. As usual, they were all untrue.

Gallacher always helped aspiring youngsters. In his new position he did his best to encourage the new leader and gave him valuable advice—and, no doubt, many words that made Duncan's ears burn.

No one could accuse Gallacher of ignoring newcomers. Sometimes, as in the case of Alex Hastings, he tried to needle them. But he could be generous, as is shown in this story told me by Bill Murray when he was Sunderland's manager : 'Once we had to field a young goalkeeper. He was dreadful, a bag of nerves. Near the end, Hughie Gallacher broke through. The match was over. We were licked and Hughie had played a big part in the result. So Hughie shouted: "Right-hand corner, sonny." Right enough, the ball went to that corner and the young fellow made a great save. Gallacher helped salvage his confidence.'

But Gallacher's time at St. James Park was running out. He was transferred to Chelsea for £10,000—a sum that made the fans of that era gasp. Gallacher was cheap at the price.

Like Law, Matthews, Best, he was a crowd-puller. When he went back to Newcastle to wear the colours of Chelsea in a League game the ground record was broken. And once when Chelsea tried to 'discipline' him by dropping him from the first eleven the gate receipts slumped by hundreds of pounds.

But the great days of Hughie Gallacher were ending. The great little man had always worn a chip on his shoulder. Now it became a rock. He became moodier, even more withdrawn. Although he had many triumphs at Stamford Bridge, and became again the idol of the crowds, he wasn't happy. Perhaps Chelsea had too many stars in those days. Perhaps there were too many cliques. Perhaps Hughie's natural reserve, his Scottish dourness, handicapped him in a club which, if not always successful, was gay, not determined enough to win every time.

And to Gallacher and nearly every other Scottish football star it was the worst crime not to worry about defeat.

Gallacher felt he needed a change. He went to Derby County. And still he could make the crowd cheer deliriously. He was as popular abroad as at home. On the Continent, where football was beginning to be appreciated, he was a sensation.

In Leipzig, where he once scored a double hat-trick, fräuleins rushed to kiss him. In Paris it was 'Vive le Gallacher'.

But Hughie was on the way down. After two seasons with Derby County, who had obtained his transfer for £3,000, he went to Notts County for £2,000, to Grimsby Town for £1,000 and, finally, to Gateshead in 1938 for £500.

Outspoken Gallacher loathed the transfer system, however, though he must have been the father of the system which involves huge fees. Once, in a newspaper article in 1938, he complained of having been 'sold like a slave for a bag of gold'.

Although £23,000 was paid for him, he didn't make a fortune out of football. His share was £60 in signing-on fees. Throughout his career he never earned more than £8 a week in the season and £6 in summer.

Yet Gallacher was a human dynamo—a man who linked artistry with uncanny ability to snatch goals and unsettle defenders. Short but sturdy, he could, with amazing speed, beat any centre-half in a race for the ball. His feints, swerves and ability to stop dead in his tracks made the crowds roar with delight at the discomfiture of his opponents.

Perhaps his greatest gift was his shooting ability.

Peter Wilson, one of Scotland's and Celtic's best winghalves, told me: 'Gallacher was astonishing in the goalmouth. In a scramble Hughie could always be relied on to get goals. He had amazing strength of leg. He could "poke" a ball into goal almost without taking a back-swing. And the ball always went with great speed.'

His record reflects that ability. In his first-class senior career Hughie Gallacher scored 386 goals. Many of them came from his lightning dash. He worked up to top pace within a few strides when he accepted a chance.

In international matches he scored twenty-eight goals—five of them against Ireland in one game and five, too, against the Irish League. His last game against England was at Hampden in 1935.

Poor Hughie! He never received the rewards he deserved from football. No Jaguar, no fancy bungalow for the wee man from Bellshill. Maybe he brooded too much. Maybe he was loved too much by the gods of football.

At the age of fifty-four Hughie Gallacher was found dead —and he died a lonely man.

But millions remember with affection and with awe the moody genius—Hughie Gallacher, the king of centre-forwards.

7

The Cheerful Earful

OF ALL the masters of Scottish football, Jimmy Mason is the most underrated. One of the reasons is that his entire senior career was spent with one club, Third Lanark. I am convinced that if Mason had been associated with a more glamorous team he would have received more international caps. Another reason is that he was one of the most pleasant, unassuming men ever to play football. While other Scottish stars were making themselves unpopular because of arrogance, a chip on their shoulders or continual condemnation of their opponents, colleagues or referees, Mason got along with everyone, loving every minute of his game, seemingly surprised that he had become a star.

I have never heard anyone in football utter a harsh word about Jimmy Mason. But how could you dislike him? He was the original happy guy, the cheerful earful of football. Oh, he could talk all right, but his flow of patter was never vicious. Even in the hottest action he could be relied on for a wisecrack that relieved the tension.

There was that torrid match in Vienna in 1951, Austria *v.* Scotland, in which Billy Steel was ordered off. Incident followed incident. Boots swung at legs, not at the ball. Suddenly a huge Austrian tangled with little Mason. When Jimmy was helped to his feet, half of his jersey had been ripped off.

Said Jimmy, deadpan, to skipper George Young: "That

bloke's lucky I didn't go after him. It was only his height that saved him.'

People still say to Jimmy: 'You're a wee comic; you should have been on the stage.' He has a Puckish humour, the wee man with the serious expression which masked one of the quickest wits in football. But there was nothing comical about his football.

Mason symbolises for me all that was perfect in the play of the unforgettable school of Scottish inside-forwards. The shrug of the shoulders that sent opponents the wrong way; the velvet touch; the superb ball-control; the accurate pass; the uncanny positional sense—Mason had them all. He made football look a simple game. If he had played for Rangers or Celtic, Arsenal or Spurs, he would, I feel, have become the most famous Scottish inside-forward of all. Certainly he deserves his place in this book, for he was in the mould of Bobby Walker and, since he retired in 1952, there has been only one player who could approach him in class and style, Ian McMillan, of Airdrie and Rangers.

Mason was Glasgow born and bred, but, as a boy, he was hardly a dedicated footballer. He had talent and he played for Haghill School, but he never dreamed football would become his career.

Indeed, when he left school he preferred to watch rather than play and he was a keen supporter of the junior Petershill, for whom his brother Archie played.

It was a shower that changed Mason's future. For weeks he had been rejecting invitations from officials of Tollcross Y.M.C.A. to turn out for them. They had heard he 'wasn't a bad inside-right'—but always Jimmy said 'No'; he preferred to watch Petershill.

One wet Saturday, however, yet another Tollcross delegation appeared at his parents' house to plead with him to play.

Jimmy looked at the weather—and decided it was better to be soaked through near home than travel away with Petershill and be drenched.

If it hadn't been for that snap decision Scotland would have lost one of the most attractive players in football history.

Soon after this Mason joined Mossvale, of Paisley, and it was there his style was formed. The fame of the little man with the distinguished feet spread. The juniors were first on his trail. Jimmy played one match, for Cambuslang Rangers, and did so well he was asked to sign.

But the juniors weren't for James Mason. As he said: 'I finished the game black and blue and I felt the junior game was too rough for me.'

Now practically every senior club in Britain were after Mason. And coming home from work—he was an apprentice brushmaker—became an ordeal for him. Desperately anxious to sign him were Arsenal, Leicester City, St. Mirren, Hibernian, Hearts, Rangers, Kilmarnock, Partick Thistle and Clyde.

Mason still recalls with awe some of the inducements offered him. Leicester suggested he should study medicine at a university and finish up Dr. James Mason.

In the end Jimmy signed for Third Lanark—on June 18th, 1936, his seventeenth birthday.

Was that a mistake? If Mason had signed for a wealthier club he would have made much more money than he did out of football and would have received international recognition earlier. But even now he is a loyal Third Lanark man and he has never forgotten the debt he owes the old Cathkin club. His wages were £4 a week—in the first team—but it was at Cathkin that he was taught his craft.

'I still had practically everything to learn about the technique of football,' he once told me. 'Up till I joined Thirds, football had been a natural game to me.'

He had never had a football lesson in his life, had never been told about positional play, how to trap the ball, how to take a throw-in or a corner, how to lift the ball or how to keep it low, how to kill a pass with chest, thigh or instep. He had played instinctively

Although he was richly endowed with talent, he quickly discovered there was much more to football in the First Division than playing it 'by ear'. There was, for instance, his left foot, which he seldom used if he could avoid it.

Mason was lucky. The manager of Third Lanark was Tom Jennings, a famous ex-centre-forward and a fine coach. He ordered Jimmy not to kick the ball with his right foot in practice for three months. 'If I shaped as if to use it,' said Jimmy, 'there was Tom beside me telling me to use my left.'

Then Mason would go round to the back of the stand— to hammer a ball against the wall and catch the rebound . . . with his left foot.

Mason was nursed carefully at Cathkin and one of his most valuable lessons was learned when he sat beside Tom Jennings at matches. 'Don't follow the ball,' the manager would tell him. 'You watch how the inside-men are playing when they haven't got the ball.' And Jimmy said afterwards he learned more in that way than he would have from playing.

Mason learned quickly and although he was only around eight stones he became a great favourite with the Cathkin enthusiasts. No wonder. In his brilliant play the spectators found a constant wellspring of delight. Although there was a delicacy and nonchalance about his style, he seemed to dominate the field, his skill and subtlety glinting through often drab company like golden sovereigns in a pouch of pennies.

A glittering career seemed certain for the wee man with the serious look and the wink in his feet. Then the war started and Mason joined up. Off he went to Gosport to a machine-gun training centre. He was invited to turn out for Portsmouth. When his regiment, the Middlesex, was moved, he played for Charlton Athletic. Even in these grim war days clubs knew all about the wee Glasgow player. Spurs and Arsenal also wanted him to play for them.

Mason was on active service for six years and when he was demobbed in 1946 he went back to Cathkin. Still his play was stamped with genius. Still he made football an art.

Still he was ignored by the Scottish selectors.

Too light, too small—these were the reasons given for failure to cap him. Mason was patient, never giving up hope that his ambition would be realised and he would play for his country.

At last the selectors saw sense. Mason was chosen to play at inside-left for the Scottish League against the League of Ireland at Ibrox on September 29th, 1948. Mason whistled. He knew that many promising careers had been wrecked in this particular representative match. But he knew, too, that he was good enough to play for his country. Although he had stayed with Third Lanark, many clubs had sought his transfer, including Charlton Athletic, Middlesbrough, Leeds United, Huddersfield Town and Hearts, so he realised, modest as he was, that he had real skill.

Mason made a glorious international début, although he was playing his third game in five days, having turned out for Third Lanark against St. Mirren on the Saturday and against Celtic in the final of the Glasgow Cup on the Monday.

This was the start of a bright new era for Scotland, for also capped for the first time in the Ibrox game were Bobby Evans, of Celtic, and Lawrie Reilly, of Hibernian, players who, with Mason, were to take the country out of the football depression into which it had fallen during and just after the war when great English teams dominated the international scene.

The following month Mason was chosen to play for a full Scotland side, against Wales at Cardiff—and he was the oldest member of the eleven. This was Mason's red-letter day in football. Again he was superb. But it is typical of the un-assuming Mason that his memory of that game is not of his own play but of another star. He says:

'We won 3—1 and it was our first post-war international success. But I'll always remember it because Willie Waddell gave one of the finest displays of right-wing play I've ever seen. Before the game Billy Steel, who was with Derby County, let me into a few secrets about chinks in the armour of the Welsh left-half and left-back. I tried out the moves and they came off. Yet it was Waddell's day. He was so de-vastating that the best laugh I had in the match was when I heard Ron Burgess and Alf Barnes arguing about who should tackle him.'

That was the start of one of the greatest Scotland partner-ships, Mason and Waddell. They fitted perfectly, reading each other's thoughts, the most brilliant post-war combination of guile and power we have seen.

Mason's greatest moment in football came in Scotland's 3—1 victory over England at Wembley in 1949. This is Jimmy's view of the game: 'It wasn't a win for Scotland, really. It was a win for our goalkeeper, Jimmy Cowan, of Morton. Jimmy made it. He took on England single-handed for the first twenty minutes and brought off some of the most amazing saves I've ever seen in my life. He inspired us, really inspired us.

'Then, suddenly, we were ahead. Billy Steel slipped the ball to Lawrie Reilly. I found I had a bit of room and I shout-ed: "Keep it low, Lawrie." And I think that shout decided big Frank Swift in the England goal to move to his right-hand post, hoping he'd be able to gobble up the ball on the deck. But Lawrie cut it back. It was a perfect pass.

'I could hear the feet of an Englishman pounding at my back, but I saw the pass coming and I saw the big goal gap to the left of Swift. I prodded the ball first time. It was a pinch, a pinch.

'Well, we won 3—1 and it was an amazing game. Wembley, you know, is always amazing. We arrived in London with no chance at all. Even the Scotsmen wouldn't back us. The bookies were laying four and five to one against us.

'Wembley is unique, though. Nothing can compare with it. When you go on to the field you feel you've go to do something special. Certainly Jimmy Cowan did it in 1949.'

Ah, but so did one James Mason. At last the wee man had really arrived. He was the toast of Scotland, hailed as the best inside-forward for years. His future was rosy—and no one deserved the break more than patient Mason.

Alas, the bad luck that dogged his career struck again.

Jimmy was picked for the Scotland eleven to play France at Hampden and booked for a tour in America in the close season.

Happily, he went along to Hampden a few days before the French game to assist in a job he loved—coaching schoolboys. Suddenly he felt a sharp pain. A few hours later he was in hospital—having his appendix removed.

There was no match against France or visit to the United States for Mason. His hoodoo had struck again.

And that was really the beginning of the end for Mason. There was still glory to come. Jimmy played several more times with distinction for Scotland. And his artistic play was now interesting foreign clubs.

In 1951 Jimmy surprised his wife when he walked into his house and said: 'We're going to Rome.' The Lazio club of

Rome had made an offer tremendous at the time: £4,000 in cash, a free house, a flight to Italy and wages of £30 a week.

I'm convinced Mason would have been the idol of the Lazio crowd, for his football was always stamped with artistry. At the time Jimmy was earning £14 a week from Third Lanark.

But he was aged thirty-two—and he liked Glasgow. So did his wife. He decided to stay at home.

Mason's great career was finishing, however. He was worried by a groin injury. Pluckily he played on, for no one loved football more than Mason. On October 18th, 1952, he pulled on the scarlet shirt of Third Lanark for the last time in the match against Motherwell.

After that game he was warned by a specialist: 'Stop playing football or you may become a cripple.' At the age of thirty-four Jimmy Mason said farewell to soccer.

To day Jimmy is a successful Glasgow businessman, still a Third Lanark fan.

In his playing career he received fourteen caps—seven for Scotland and seven for the Scottish League. He would have been even more successful if it hadn't been for the war. He would have earned more from football if he had signed for one of the wealthy clubs who wanted him.

But he wouldn't have been the Mason I revered if he had gone elsewhere. He was a football genius, combining in his play a unique blend of skill, experience and character.

There was wit in his play as well as the touch of velvet. Most of all he had poise. Like so many great Scottish inside-forwards, he always seemed mature, older than his years. He invariably did the right thing at the right time. He was never brash, never rash. Few I've seen ever had the composure of Jimmy Mason.

He always seemed to have time in hand—and that's the hallmark of the Scottish inside-man.

Today there's little true artistry. Football has turned into a hurricane; speed is too often all.

Would there be room now for a man like Jimmy Mason? I don't know. I don't care. He was a hero of his time, his play bathed in glorious autumn colours, deep, impressive, haunting.

And how I wish I could see players of his talent in this era. His game was always pure and sweet and clean.

8

The Wee Blue Devil

THIS is what Arnold Bennett said of football in his novel *The Card*: ' "But I don't see what football has got to do with being mayor." She endeavoured to look like a serious politician. "You are nothing but a cuckoo," Dentry pleasantly informed her. "Football has got to do with everything." '

Bennett was right. Football, especially in Scotland, has not only got to do with everything; it is practically everything. It is love, hate, career, religion. It is, for the true fan, too serious to be called a hobby. It is a passion.

How does one become involved in football? Why does one become a fanatic?

I know why I did. It was because of Alan Morton.

I was very young and just starting to support my local club, Kilmarnock. I was taken to Ibrox to see Kilmarnock play Rangers. And it was then that football took a grip on me that has persisted to this day.

I can never forget that magic moment. The scene might have been painted by Walt Disney. It was a day of gold and blue and the pitch was as green as an Irish exile's dream of home. And then I saw Morton in action for the first time. He was poetry in motion. He darted almost contemptuously past the Kilmarnock defenders. His crosses were perfection.

I gazed, entranced. I had never seen anyone as perfect.

Here was glamour, here was romance, here was a real hero, a dapper little man in blue with sleek hair and the poise of a ballet dancer.

That scene lives with me today as vividly as it did all those years ago. Morton on the ball—that, I had found, was really what football was about. And I have seen nothing since, despite studying most of the masters in the past thirty-five years, to equal the skill and grace of Alan Morton dancing down the left wing.

Even the English realised Morton was a football genius and they were not grudging in their praise. This is what was said of the Ranger in *Association Football*:

'There was not much of Morton in height—about five feet five inches—but what there was was well built and his body moved on a strong pair of limbs bottomed by feet both of which wielded a powerful shot and which, in unison, could baffle the cutest of opponents. He had perfect balance. Even before he reached the height of his career as a professional, he was to England what Matthews became to Scotland, a holy terror. Man after man was fielded by the English selectors in an effort to solve what was actually an insoluble puzzle. England even thought up one that was unique: they tried the experiment of playing against him a half-back of Morton's own dimensions. The man they picked on was Magee of West Bromwich Albion, but he proved as ineffective as those before him and the others after him.'

Morton was a football genius. There had never been anything like him before in Scotland as an outside-left; there is nothing to approach him in the game today and it is very questionable if there ever will be.

He had every trick and was a master in the art of ball control. It was near impossible to divine his intentions, he could so effectively change his mind, his direction of travel, in a split second. All sorts of ways were employed in an effort to put a stopper on him, from bull-rushing at him to laying off, but all with the same result—Morton reached his objective. He could raise spectators to the highest pitch of excitement, he could make them roar with joy, he could make them laugh with the sheer achievement of the seemingly impossible and he could make them feel sorry for the 'other fellow'. He was the essence of sportsmanship, and was never once guilty of an underhand action.

Aye, that was Morton to a T. A holy terror. The original wee blue devil. It is of Morton that the most famous of all football jingles sings: 'Oh, Charlie Shaw, he never saw where Alan Morton pit the ba'.'

There is no doubt that Alan Morton was the greatest left-winger who ever played for Scotland and Rangers. Some believe he was the greatest winger, right or left, of all time, an even better player than Stanley Matthews. You can argue all day and all night about that. But it is an argument that will never be settled. What *is* true beyond all doubt, however, is that Morton's goal-scoring exploits put Matthews, the maker, seldom the taker, of goals, completely in the shade.

The goals scored by Morton have become legends, for they were among the most remarkable in the long history of football because they were scored by a craftsman, whose hours of prodigious practice had made him an expert. Sometimes the goals looked like flukes. They weren't, for Morton was one of the few players who could, like an expert golfer, slice or hook the ball, give it spin as well as direct it with the accuracy and speed of an arrow shot by Robin Hood.

His greatest goal had one of Scotland's most magnificent goalkeepers, Jimmy Brownlie, blushing. The burly keeper muttered fiercely under his breath as he bent dejectedly to pick the ball from the back of the Third Lanark net. Brownlie was a superb exponent of the goalkeeper's art, a model for the great keepers who came after him, but even he had been made to look silly. Cathkin buzzed as the goal was scored. 'Fluke,' bellowed the disconsolate Third Lanark supporters. And even the grinning Rangers fans felt there had been more than a trace of luck about the goal.

But two Rangers players knew the goal had really been planned. They were the scorer, Alan Morton, and the Ibrox left-half, Tully Craig.

Rangers had been awarded a free kick on a spot between the penalty line and the touchline, only ten yards from the bye-line. Tully Craig came up to take the kick. Alan remarked, jokingly: 'Do you want to see a goal?' Craig smiled. 'Bet you a bob you don't score.' Alan carefully placed the ball. But it seemed impossible that a goal could be scored, for the angle was so acute that it seemed that only a lob in front of the keeper would be profitable.

But Morton ran forward and kicked the ball with his right foot. Away soared the ball, zooming towards the far post. Brownlie braced himself, then relaxed. He was sure the ball was going past.

Then—it suddenly swung in the air. It took a banana curve, swerved in and went past Brownlie into the net, high up.

It looked like magic.

The most famous goal scored by Morton was that one which started the 'Charlie Shaw' chant. It was in one of the palpitating battles at Parkhead between the Old Firm, Celtic and Rangers, in the golden days of these matches.

Morton was out on his wing. He received a pass and cut in swiftly. But he ran into a block of defenders. There was only one thing to do. He swept the ball out to his own position, which he knew instinctively would be filled by a colleague. Right enough, Tommy Cairns was there. But he, too, faced a formidable barrier of defenders. So he whipped the ball back to Morton almost at once.

There seemed little Morton could do. He was caught on the wrong foot and the pass had been hit too hard. Everyone, and certainly Charlie Shaw, the great Celtic goalkeeper of the time, expected Alan to swing wildly with his left foot or try to trap the ball before parting with it. Instead, Alan allowed the ball to pass his right side and then he drove at it with all he had—again with his right foot.

It was a wonderful goal and again it looked like magic.

But there was no magic, no luck, about these goals, Morton said long afterwards. The goals came merely because, as a youngster, he had practised and practised until taking shots from all angles and with either foot had become a simple affair for him.

And now let the great winger himself tell how he practised for this is the best advice I have ever heard given in football to any aspiring youngsters. Certainly the Alan Morton story is an inspiration to any boy who wants to become a star. It was sheer hard work which took Alan Morton to the pinnacle of fame. Listen to him, read the words of golden advice over and over again, you lads who seek to emulate him, then go out and put what he has told you into effect.

Here, then, is the Alan Morton formula for football success:

'There are three essentials for any young fellow who wants to become a footballer—balance, control and quickness off the mark. It has been said that I possessed these virtues, but if they were revealed in my play they came to me only by intensive practice. But practice must never be a labour. It must be a love and that was what it always was to me.

'As a youth, I took a ball into the back garden and there, for hours, I practised. Behind our house and positioned in the back garden was a wooden door through which coal was emptied into the cellar. The door was about four feet from ground level and in its centre was an opening just big enough to take a football. That was my target.

'I aimed to put the ball through that aperture. Of course, it didn't always work out that way. Sometimes, indeed, I didn't want a bull's-eye. It was often better when the ball came back from the wall at different angles. This meant that as the ball shot back off the wall I found myself forced to meet the return with either foot.

'Gradually I found myself kicking the ball in the direction I wanted. Proficiency came slowly but in a way that became natural the longer I kept at it. At first, it was all deliberate, but later it became almost automatic, a reflex action.

'Time meant nothing. I would hit the ball with my right foot. It would rebound from the wall at great speed, forcing me to anticipate its flight and make me dash to the other end of the lawn to meet it, this time with my left foot.

'This not only developed speed in gathering the ball but control in direction and in placing it to the mark. When I became a player I felt no difficulty in meeting a running ball and sending it where I wanted with either foot. All so vital in disorganising a defence.

'If a defence is to be beaten, no time must be given to let the backs take up position to meet the attack. Consider—if, once an opening has been made and the defenders caught off balance, a delay by me in crossing the ball, with my colleagues up and ready to meet it, could enable a defender to travel eight to ten yards in a second. So you can see how vital it is to get a moving ball over with either foot without having to stop it first, thereby braking the attack and giving the defenders a chance they shouldn't be getting.'

One of Alan Morton's most famous tricks was to pivot

suddenly on the bye-line and curl the ball to the far post, there to be met by one of his colleagues, or—and this happened often—to find the net of its own volition.

According to Alan, who became a director of the club he served so well, that tactic, too, could be traced back to his days of constant practice in the back garden with an old ball and the hole in the door.

He also says : 'It isn't only the foot that is actually kicking the ball which gets the full results; it is where you put the other to secure perfect pivoting. You must always ensure that, no matter how you may be forced to turn to meet the break of the ball, you are balanced in such a way that you can secure the direction wanted with ease and without strain.'

This advice applies to other sports. Alan Morton was not only a great footballer. He was a formidable opponent for the best on the golf links, where his balance was also perfect.

On football, Alan adds :

'With time vital, you must be able to use either foot as the ball comes to you, often with an unexpected swerve. If you aren't poised comfortably, hesitancy will result and a chance will be lost.

'Quickness in movement and in execution is the most defence-deceiving trick in the game. The little subtle moves as a schoolboy should still be with you as a senior. Say a winger makes what appears an orthodox manœuvre. The back instinctively goes the way he believes the winger means to move when the ball reaches him.

'But if the winger can suddenly and without stopping flick the ball in the opposite direction from the path the back is taking, he can open up a way through which he may be able to travel unopposed.

'It's like carpentry. A joiner is troubled when he has to go against the grain of the wood. It's the same in football for if you compel a back to go against the grain, or direction, you have him struggling and that is half the battle won.'

These are the wise words of Alan Morton, one of the most articulate of footballers, who always wants to see youth break through. 'But,' he once told me, 'you must have a stout heart. You must expect heartbreak before you reach the goal you have made for yourself.' Certainly Morton suffered many disappointments before he was accepted as a star.

His first dream was to play for Airdrieonians. He was born in Glasgow but went to Shotts when his father, a mining engineer, moved there with his family. In 1910 he played as a schoolboy for the Rest of Scotland against Glasgow. He began to study mining engineering soon after he had left Airdrie Academy. Soon he was playing in juvenile football with his brother, R. M. Morton, who became a well-known centre-forward with Queen's Park.

Alan thought his ambition had been realised when the Airdrie manager, John Chapman, asked him to play in a benefit game at Broomfield. By this time he was a left-winger, although he had played at centre-forward as a schoolboy. He was disappointed when he was told to play at centre-forward against Motherwell and not in his new and favourite position, on the wing. Still, he scored a goal and felt he had done well. He even thought Airdrie might ask him to sign.

Alas, no one ever asked him to join up at Broomfield.

Which, even Airdrie will agree, was probably the miss of the century by a senior club.

Then Queen's Park became interested in the Morton brothers and the great Glasgow amateur club soon had Alan and Bob in their second eleven.

Again Alan discovered that fame wasn't to arrive overnight.

He thought he had made his first-team place secure; then he was told: 'You could do with more experience.'

Alan felt gloomy, but the Queen's Park committee changed their minds and after Alan had scored a glorious goal against Third Lanark—yes, the famous Jimmy Brownlie was again the goalkeeper beaten by Morton's fine shot—he was well on the way to the stars.

Soon the international selectors spotted him. The 1914–18 war prevented him receiving international honours earlier, but after its close he was chosen by both the S.F.A. and the Scottish League. For the League he played in 1919 in the two unofficial matches against England, on April 26th and May 3rd, and one against Ireland on March 22nd, 1919. Full international honours came his way when he was capped against Wales and Ireland in 1920. He was also chosen that year to play against England, but he was forced to withdraw because of injury.

Alan Morton had arrived and soon Rangers were on his trail. In 1920 he became a professional footballer, joining a Rangers team which was soon to become one of the greatest the country has ever seen.

Now we can come to the hub of the matter. What makes a football star, what's inside a master of the sport? Morton shows it best of all. Natural ability, determination, continual practice—all these play a part. But there is something just as important: a stout heart which laughs at setbacks.

If you study the stories of our football immortals you will find for most of them the way to the top was anything but smooth. That they weren't dismayed by setbacks, rebuffs is a tribute to their courage, confidence and grit—and it should be an example to all aspiring stars.

Football life wasn't all ham for Morton. Not even when he joined Rangers. He seemed to have reached the heights, he had become a member of one of the greatest clubs in the world, he was an internationalist.

But Alan lived for two months in a nightmare. He couldn't find his real form at Ibrox. The critics complained—as they still complain today about new Rangers players: 'Ach, that Alan Morton! A' richt fur Queen's, mebbe. But he's oot o' his class wi' the 'Gers.'

What was wrong? Alan wasn't sure. So he practised harder than ever, every spare moment he had being devoted to attempts to tame the ball.

Still he failed to hit it off.

Until he realised he had been trying to do too much.

He had been trying to play as he thought a professional should. So there was one thing to do. Alan did it.

He reverted to his natural game. And soon his famous partnership with Tommy Cairns was the pride of Ibrox.

It wasn't long before Alan became the idol of the very fans who had been criticising him. Characteristically, he paid tribute to his partner: 'I can never adequately express my thanks to Tommy Cairns for all he did for me during my long association with him.'

Alan was lucky in his inside-forwards, with whom he was exceedingly popular. No wonder. He was the dream partner for any inside man.

But sometimes his partners weren't popular with the crowds.

There was, for example, an international at Parkhead. Critics complained that Jimmy McMenemy, of Celtic, his inside partner, 'starved' Morton. What they didn't know was that Alan had been taken ill soon after the game began and had asked Jimmy to play as much as possible to the right wing.

This the famous McMenemy did—and caught it in the neck from Morton admirers.

Tommy Cairns was also blamed for failing to give Morton a proper service in his first international against Wales at Cardiff in 1920. Again the critics failed to appreciate what was going on during the match.

The astute Cairns knew that Morton was up against two of the hardest-hitting defenders who ever played for Wales, Fred Keenor and Moses Russell, and he felt that if he continued to play to his little winger Alan wouldn't get much chance in his first international. So Cairns took over all the heavy work and played more to the centre or to the right wing. And afterwards Alan made it clear how much he appreciated Tommy's policy.

Alan Morton made football history. Before he finished his career and became a Rangers director in 1933-4, he played in 495 games and scored 115 goals in his thirteen seasons with the Ibrox club. He had a total of ninety-two caps and medals.

The stories about the famous Ranger with the sense of humour are countless. One of the best was when Alan, always a leg-puller, bet Kenny Campbell, the Partick Thistle goalkeeper, that he would score against him at Firhill.

'All right,' said Kenny, 'I'll bet you a pound box of chocolates you don't.'

Sure enough, Alan scored a goal. After the match Campbell said : 'I'll send on your pound box.'

Morton laughed : 'Thanks. But be sure it's a pound sterling box of chocolates.'

Let us end the Morton story with a question : How would Alan Morton compare with Stanley Matthews? That's a poser which can never be answered. But I once listened to David Meiklejohn, one of soccer's greatest players, a wonderful Rangers half-back who played so often with Alan Morton, talk about that subject when he was manager of Partick Thistle.

'Morton and Matthews,' he said, 'had much in common. Neither relied on sheer speed as their main attributes to bring them success. Their stride in running was as different as night is from day, but each could claim great velocity over a twenty-five-yard stretch. They were not slow, of course, over a greater distance, but it was rather their artistry, not mere fleetness of foot, which brought them world fame.

'Alan had a swerve that could deceive the best and a cross that mesmerised many a goalkeeper. But his great attribute, I think, was his ability to beat a back on the inside and let go a fierce drive with his right foot. That is one feature where I say Alan was better than Stan—he could score goals with either his right or his left foot.

'Both had uncanny poise and balance. Who was the better? Let me put it this way: two grand players to have in your side . . . but a damned nuisance if you were playing against them.'

9

The Mighty Atom

EVEN Willie Maley had doubts. He looked again at the slight
lad with the spindly, pencil-thin legs wearing a green-and-
white jersey that reached below his knees, sighed and tried
to shut out the jeers of the Celtic supporters.

'Awa' hame tae yer maw!' bellowed one wit. 'Ye'll get the
cruelty men after ye!' shouted another. 'Puir wee soul, you'll
get killed!' cried a third.

A director turned to the great manager and snapped: 'What
did I tell you? That boy's not nearly strong enough for senior
football.' And for once Celtic's strong man looked glum.
Could his judgment have been wrong? Had he been too dogmatic, too clever? Certainly he confessed afterwards: 'I was
very unhappy. I felt I had backed a loser. And never did I see
anyone less like a professional footballer.'

But as he sat back to watch the game he recalled all the
glowing reports he had heard of Patsy Gallacher, the frail
seventeen-year-old who didn't seem at all worried by the
crowd's laughter, glared at his director and snorted: 'We'll
just wait and see.'

And what Celtic saw that afternoon had even the most
doubting of their fans cheering wildly at the end—cheering
the wisp of 5 ft. 6 in. and a little over seven stones in weight.

For in his opening appearance for Celtic, in a friendly game
at Dumfries in season 1910–11, on a pitch as soggy as a bride's

first cake, the magic of Patsy Gallacher glittered like the fairy lights on a Christmas tree.

Only once again did fans laugh at Gallacher. That was when he ran out to play his first big game for Celtic at home, against St. Mirren. Again the laughter was stilled abruptly when Gallacher touched the ball. From that moment on he became the hero of Parkhead and undoubtedly one of the most fascinating, most entertaining and most brilliant inside-forwards of all time.

Was he the greatest? Celtic chairman Bob Kelly has no doubts. 'Patsy Gallacher was the best player I ever saw, unexcelled as a ball-worker and dribbler, always direct in his approach to goal, and gifted with an uncanny facility of changing speed in one stride.' And these words are echoed by Willie Maley, the man who knew Patsy best, and who wrote in his *The Story of Celtic*, in 1939: 'I will say without any fear of contradiction that there never was one who gave better service to the club and with so little to commend him in the way of physique.'

He was past his peak when I first saw him, but even then he was still adept at trailing the ball upfield, cutely inviting a tackle and, having coaxed several opponents round him, suddenly switching the ball into an open space to one of his well-placed colleagues. Even then, too, his ball-juggling was the wonder of all the soccer world and I'm convinced that Stanley Matthews himself could not have taught him anything.

As far as I am concerned, however, Patsy is supreme in one respect. There is no greater inspiration to any youngster who wants to make good than the Gallacher story.

It is true that some of our greatest footballers haven't really looked like athletes. Indeed, when you met them off the field you could hardly believe they were star players. Some have been small and frail, others have been beanpole slim.

And not a few looked as though they should have been on a diet.

But no one has shown as Patsy Gallacher did that you don't need physique to be a soccer genius.

So if you're worried about your lack of height, thinness of thigh or calf, absence of muscle or weight, remember Patsy Gallacher.

Although he was born in Donegal, he was brought to Scotland by his parents early in life. All his magic was displayed to Scots and that is why I feel he must be included in any gallery of Scottish football masters.

Patsy's early days were spent in Renfrew and his first club was the local Juvenile Renfrew St. James. Soon stories of the fragile laddie who had magic in his boots reached Clydebank Juniors, one of the top teams in those days, and they lost no time in signing him. With the junior club Patsy earned new fame and the seniors were attracted, but as soon as the scouts saw the puny boy they shook their heads and decided that he could not stand up to the rigours of league football.

His ability was never in doubt—and that was the factor which Willie Maley thought most about.

Patsy was a seventeen-year-old carpenter at John Brown's shipyard when he joined Celtic. Said Maley afterwards: 'He was probably the dirtiest-faced player ever to grace the turf at Parkhead. He used to come running from his work at the shipyard without time to wash before a match. But he was also the best dirty-faced player we ever had!'

Always a bright, agile player, Patsy became a Celtic Park hero in an amazingly short time. Within a month of signing, he had made sure of his place in the first team and in another three months he had won a Scottish Cup medal.

At this time, the little inside-forward looked on himself as a football apprentice—and his shipyard chums looked on

Jimmy McMullan, the
great Scottish skipper

George Stevenson

David Meiklejohn

Jimmy McGrory with a Celtic star of today, Bertie Auld

Opposite, Jim Baxter in a happy mood after Rangers' triumph

Bob McPhail with a great Englishman, Blenkinsop

Opposite, Sammy Cox

Bobby Evans

Law hails Baxter after a Wembley goal

him as an eccentric—for he spent his meal hour practising
with a ball on his own instead of joining in the kick-abouts.

If Patsy lacked muscle, he had plenty of heart. At the start
of his career, before he grew strong and sinewy, his apparent
frailness encouraged many opponents, unable to cope with
his feints and dodges, to resort to tactics that were meant to
frighten him. Patsy wasn't worried. He anticipated every
move, every intention, could read a rival's mind and many a
surprised opponent had the shock of his life when a com-
pact little mass hit him square and fair—and flattened
him.

Nevertheless, Gallacher suffered from the attentions of un-
scrupulous opponents—and there were real giants in those
days. As far back as Patsy's heyday, there was the moan that is
with us today: not enough protection is given by referees to
ball players. It was his strong opinion, especially in his early
days, that referees failed to give him due protection and even
he couldn't always avoid ferocious tackles. He made up his
mind to fight his own battles—and, as he once said grimly,
'I've seldom failed.'

Patsy, of course, must have been a tantalising little beggar
to opponents, for he had the knack of playing right on to a
defender's feet, then gliding past quickly, making the other
look foolish. That often meant rash retaliation. But Patsy's
pluck was amazing, his stamina astounding. He never lacked
grit; never lost his ability to fight to the last second, for no
game was ever lost for him until the final whistle sounded.
And certainly I never heard of any defender who could boast
he had the mighty atom 'tied up' in any match.

Soon Patsy Gallacher was becoming a legend. 'The Mighty
Atom' was only one of his nicknames. He was also called
'Peerless Patsy', 'The Wonderful Midget', and he was to
football what Jimmy Wilde was to boxing.

G

His admirers said that he could do anything on the field that any other great player could do—and also do things that only a Patsy Gallacher would have attempted. He scored many magnificent goals, laid on hundreds for his colleagues. But he was the complete inside-forward.

His individualistic genius is recalled by one of the most superb goals ever scored in Scotland.

It was the Scottish Cup Final of 1924–5. Celtic were playing Dundee—and time was running out for the Glasgow club. Playing brilliant football, Dundee were leading 1—0. Inspired by Gallacher, Celtic fought back. But the Dundee defence seemed impregnable. Then Patsy had the ball and off he darted, beating opponent after opponent. He twisted. He turned. He feinted. He bored. And now he was in the goal area and there was panic at last among the defenders. And there was a mighty crash and Patsy was on his knees a yard from goal and the greatest scrum known in Cup Final history was heaving on top of him.

But one figure emerged from the scramble—a diminutive figure. It was Gallacher and he had the ball wedged between his skinny legs and, hopping, almost somersaulting, he landed the ball and himself in the net.

It was a fitting climax to an astounding exhibition of pure unadulterated skill and pluck and all Hampden went mad and even the Dundee players had difficulty in refraining from applauding. After that Celtic just couldn't lose. Jimmy Mc-Grory scored the winner. But it was the equaliser that was always talked about afterwards and that goal illustrates what was probably Gallacher's most notable asset—his contempt of odds, no matter how great. Indeed, his bravery on the field almost amounted to recklessness.

His affection for his club and his determination to ensure that teamwork always came first are recalled by this story told by Peter Wilson, who played behind Patsy at right-half and became one of the most polished middlemen in Scotland.

'Patsy had a mind of his own on the field. And he could impose it on colleague and opponent alike. Although he was such a supreme individualist, he was so brilliant that he could combine with any kind of player. He really believed in team-work and his individual darts and dribbles were made only when he felt nothing else would work.

'Anyhow, I recall one match in which I played behind him when I was seventeen. I got the ball at mid-field and found myself beating one opponent, two opponents. I'm in the mood, I told myself. And I ran on and beat another defender. Now I was in shooting range and I let go. The ball flew into the net and I threw my hands in the air joyfully and looked for my mates to congratulate me.

'The first man I reached was Patsy. I thrust out my hand. But Patsy glared at me. "Get back to your kennel," he snapped, "and make sure you stay there. It's us yins up front that do the scoring."

'And that was the first real lesson I learned in the art of team-work.'

Gallacher was at home in any of the forward positions—and such was his versatility, his supreme command of the football craft, that he once had an outstanding game at centre-half. Certainly he had one of the quickest-thinking brains football has known and although he was prone to snort and snap like a terrier at an inquisitive mastiff he usually exercised extraordinary control over his temper even when exasperated opponents went over the score to get their own back on the little man who had diddled them.

Gallacher revelled in playing with colleagues of outstanding class. I have been told by veteran writers that one of the greatest displays of entertaining soccer ever seen was at a

Glasgow-Sheffield game at Hampden when Gallacher and Alan Morton played in the same forward line, showed their inimitable touches, and made the Sheffield men, all players of high calibre, look like novices.

Honours, of course, fell thickly on the little man. He won four Scottish Cup medals, seven League Championship medals, eleven Glasgow Charity Cup medals and four Glasgow Cup medals. He was capped thirteen times for his native country and the Scottish League also honoured him; but there is no doubt that if he had been of Scottish birth Patsy would seldom have been out of the Scotland team.

He also had a unique distinction for a player whose heart always lay at Parkhead: he was once a Rangers player—and by special request. It was for Andy Cunningham's benefit game. And he received another tribute to his ability and personality when the Scottish League departed from its usual practice and sponsored a League eleven to play in a Patsy Gallacher benefit.

In season 1925-6, after fifteen years at Parkhead, Celtic felt the little forward had reached the end of his career as far as first-class football was concerned and they released him. Falkirk stepped in and signed him and, with his change of jersey, Patsy switched his style—and became the best bargain the Bairns of Brockville ever made.

Gallacher turned into a general who introduced a new technique to Falkirk, contriving the situations, making the passes and letting his colleagues do the shooting. Falkirk didn't win any honours during the time Gallacher was with them, but they had many moments of glory and they cultivated a type of football which brought new life and vigour to the game in Stirlingshire.

Patsy spent six years at Falkirk before he retired. He became a successful businessman. He died in 1953.

Those who were privileged to see him will never forget his greatness in the arts and crafts of football, his high courage and the self-imposed discipline. He also had a sense of humour and the story is told that after he had played for Rangers in Cunningham's benefit game, Sir John Ure Primrose, then chairman of the Ibrox club, entered the dressing-room and congratulated the wee man on a fine goal he had scored for Rangers. Patsy looked up, grinned and said: 'Maybe you'll no' be thinking the same way, Sir John, if I score the same sort of goal against Rangers in our next match.'

His old friends said of Patsy Gallacher that he was a quiet, shy, unassuming little man, embarrassed at the recollection by others of his football genius, who found happiness in a spirit of charity and goodwill to all.

Certainly he was a modest man. A few years before he died I asked him what he thought about modern inside-forwards. He shook his head. 'Who am I to criticise?' he said. 'I was lucky. I think I had the gift for football. I believe you either have it or you haven't. The lads today do their best and they're bigger and fitter and faster. I don't think, though, they're as skilful as some of the men in the old days. And I wasn't the best, you know. Oh, no. Maybe I could hold my own in dribbling with any. But I couldn't shoot, for instance, like Andy Cunningham did. And I always felt that J. B. McAlpine, of Queen's Park—"Mutt" he used to be called—was a classic inside-forward.'

I pressed him. 'What do you think is wrong with the present-day inside-men?' 'I'll be frank, then,' said Patsy. 'The shooting facility is lacking today. You see, men like Cunningham, Bob McPhail, Willie Buchan, Tim Dunn, Lachie McMillan, Charlie Napier and George Stevenson could shoot as well as play brilliantly. I often wish I had packed a shot like Andy Cunningham.'

But Patsy was being too modest. He could hit them as venomously as any of his great contemporaries. And not one of the others could work the ball as Patsy did. He was the most spectacular and certainly the greatest one-man band football has ever known—an entertainer as well as a fine team man.

Some have called him the Matthews of his era. I prefer to call Matthews the Gallacher of his age. That's how good he was. And certainly, when you consider the strange facts, Gallacher and Matthews had much in common—the brooding expression, the thin face, the prominent nose, the thought they put into the game—even though they played in widely varying epochs.

But often they played the same role for the sides—the role of the one hero conducting the fortunes of their colleagues, which is one of the most warming spectacles in the whole of sport. Such was Gallacher's domination of Celtic and Falkirk and Matthews's of Blackpool and Stoke that you half expected to see them handing out the lemons at half-time.

Their trademark was the havoc they caused, the fields littered with bodies of opponents who had tried vainly to stop their dazzling forays.

They were unlikely-looking athletes, Gallacher and Matthews, but no greater footballers have ever illuminated the green, green grass of British pitches.

I wonder how they would have fared if they had played in the same team? No, I wonder how opponents would have fared. But that thought is enough to give the greatest of modern defenders a nightmare.

10

Man of Many Faces

IT WAS like a boiler bursting—the sigh of relief that went soaring into the soft, warm, autumn night at Ibrox.

Rangers were playing Red Star of Belgrade in a European Cup-tie and once again the Glasgow team were finding it difficult to pierce a packed defence. There were only precious seconds to go. Suddenly Jim Baxter had the ball. With time ticking away there was only one thing to do. And, almost subconsciously, master footballer Baxter did it. In vivid contrast to his usual fascinating flick or gentle glide he booted the ball—really booted it. Hard. High.

A flickering blob under the blazing floodlights, the ball curved down. And goalkeeper Dujkovic, who had been so competent all that September night of 1964, was caught napping. He blundered and in nipped Ralph Brand to score. Rangers' pressure had paid off and the fans sighed gustily as their team won the first leg by 3—1, the last goal making a world of difference in the torrid European tournament.

To Ralph Brand went the glory of scoring. But the man who really won the tie for Rangers was James Baxter, the man of many faces, the player who has all the style and grace of the old-timers and the imaginative ideas of the moderns, one of the most fascinating footballers of all time.

After the game I asked Baxter, a cheerful extrovert, why he had swung the ball high—a move unusual for him. Jim looked at me in amazement. 'Nothing else I could dae, sir,' he said. 'I kent the goalie would miss it. I'd sized him up.'

And there was nothing boastful about that remark. Baxter had, indeed, summed up the keeper's strengths—and weaknesses. Instinctively, he had known just what to do, realised the goalkeeper had a fatal flaw—and gambled on a deceptive lob.

You can't help liking Baxter, although, like the goalkeeper he had so carefully assessed, Jim, too, has weaknesses as well as strengths.

As a player, he is a charmer—entrancing, football poetry in motion. He has an impish sense of humour—but he also hates to lose, he loves to take the mickey out of opponents and referees and he likes, overmuch, I feel, to be boss. But as a captain he is an enigma. I had hoped that the many faces of Baxter, known to his friends as Stanley, to the fans as Slim, had merged one day in November 1964 into the image to be accepted as the real Jim. That was when he captained Scotland for the first time in a full international against Ireland at Hampden. And he showed he had the stature, the command and the dedication to make for himself a reputation as one of the great Scottish skippers.

Perhaps Baxter can still be a valiant Scottish captain—if he puts his mind to it.

But I have the feeling that Baxter is too skilled a player to make the ideal skipper. Also he's too much of a wag. He's the guy in the Fife coalfield, in John Brown's shipyard, in Kilmarnock's Glenfield and Kennedy, in the Motherwell steelworks—the guy with the flamboyant touch, the wisecrack, the colour—the guy who cocks a snook at authority . . . and usually gets away with it.

Too often he can't control his eccentric genius. Now and again his inherent unruliness breaks through and he reminds

you of the wartime sergeant who lost his stripes mainly because he really only wanted to be one of the squad. I don't
think authority is what this somewhat off-beat character who
seeks adventure wants.

But Jim Baxter doesn't appear in this book because of his
command as a captain. He is here because he is a master of
football, a great master, and no matter what some people think
of him there is no doubt in my mind that he is one of the most
attractive and skilful players who has ever kicked a ball.

He has been called a soccer scientist and to see him pierce
and probe the opposition is one of the game's modern miracles. He tames the other team with contemptuous flick, wriggle
of hip or shrug of slim shoulders. He holds the ball artistically
then shows touches of Pele and Kopa and Di Stefano as he
makes the pass, the run or the feint. He is an instinctive player,
doing the right thing at the right time.

And he hasn't changed all that much—in style, that is—
since he was signed for Crossgates Primrose, the Fife side,
in 1955.

The man who signed him, Primrose secretary Willie
Butchart, says:

'Jim devoured every word when we were discussing tactics.
But you couldn't tell him how to play. He played it his way.
He just couldn't play it any other way and how could you
argue with a boy who had so much talent?

'He was like a king ruling the course of a match. He was
always the boy you had your eye on. You stopped chatting
when Baxter was on the ball. He didn't tackle much and I
didn't blame him for he was like a skeleton then, not a pick
of flesh on him. But what a player.'

Today Jim isn't as thin, has grown more sophisticated.
He's a great learner and not so long ago he told me how embarrassed he had been when he arrived in Glasgow to join

the first representative Scottish side for which he had been picked—an under twenty-three eleven. 'I thought I was a killer in dress,' he grinned. 'But what a suit I was wearing. I'd had it specially made in Fife. And then I met boys from London and Manchester all dolled up in mohair and the latest styles. I felt like hiding.'

Jim took the lesson. Now he is one of football's best-dressed men.

But he still plays football his way. Why not? Critics sneer that Baxter isn't really a team man, too much of an individualist, still can't tackle, of little use when things are going badly. That criticism is unfair. Baxter is as brave a player as any and he still believes that sheer football talent will out. His real handicap is that he is sometimes too sharp, a move ahead of slower-thinking colleagues, caught out because another player hasn't anticipated his pass or move into another position. He is a natural. He would have stood out in the old days; he is as adept in the current method football, in which he controls the middle of the field, as he would have been in the outmoded W formation.

There is no better passer in the game today than the genius from Fife, who is sometimes arrogant, sometimes foolish but who has stamped his personality on football in a way no one else has done since the days of James, Jackson and Gallacher.

Greatness and controversy have surrounded him for years. When he broke his leg playing for Rangers against Vienna Rapid it was almost a national disaster. When he married it rated front-page news. When he was transferred from Rangers to Sunderland for around £70,000 in May 1965 the arguments among Scottish fans raged for weeks.

But I have never found Baxter to be big-headed. He is a great kidder and likes to take the mickey out of reporters as much as he likes to rib opponents and referees. He is, however, a cheerful companion, generous to a fault, a shrewd Fifer who has never been upset by headlines, praise or criticism.

In many ways Baxter's is the classic story of the country boy who made good.

No one ever dreamed that Jim Baxter, born in Hill o' Beath, Fife, on September 29th, 1939, would become a national figure. He was the only child of Mr. and Mrs. Baxter. His father was a miner and Jim followed in his footsteps, first down the mine, then as a footballer.

Unlike Denis Law and other notable Scottish players, Baxter showed no early genius at the game. He was good but not brilliant—and the scouts who saw him early in his career considered he was too skinny and too tall ever to make a prospect.

Willie Butchart, however, always had faith in Jim, so much so that he paid the lanky genius 10s. a week whether he was in the team or not.

Butchart has said: 'I always had a hunch about Jim. I saw him playing for Hill o' Beath Boys' Club, who trained at Humbug Park, the ground of our junior team, Crossgates Primrose, now, alas, defunct.

'I don't remember ever being so keen to sign a youngster as I was about Baxter and as well as the £2 10s. signing-on fee we gave him £30, with which, by the way, he bought his mother a washing machine.'

Baxter was sixteen when he played for Primrose and for a long time it seemed that only Willie Butchart considered the lad had talent. The only club to offer him a trial as a senior were Raith Rovers. Again Jim's luck was in; the trial, against Rangers reserves in 1957, brought him to the notice of another character, bluff Bert Herdman, then manager of Raith Rovers.

Bert signed Baxter for £200. 'That was money well spent,' said Herdman. 'I have no doubt that Baxter is the greatest player there has been in Scotland in the past thirty years.'

Now Baxter, who had started as a left-winger, was at left-half and the chance Rovers had taken in signing him began to pay off. Already he was making friends and enemies—mainly because of his astonishing confidence. It was Jim's confidence that impressed Bert Herdman. And the Rovers' manager's words should be heeded even now by Baxter critics who don't fancy his approach to football. Bert's view is:

'There's no harm in a man like Baxter thinking that he's good. That only makes him even better. I liked Jim's unbounded confidence right from the start.'

It was in season 1958–9 that Baxter's name began to be mentioned in higher circles.

In one memorable game at Starks Park, the ground of Raith Rovers, Baxter played against Rangers.

Rangers fans couldn't believe it. Who was this lad Baxter? He looked as though a gust of wind would blow him over, seemed a frail stripling compared with the Ibrox stalwarts. But what a player! He teased and tormented Rangers players, had them running round in circles and was the main reason Raith Rovers had one of their best if most surprising victories, 3—1.

A few months after this Jim was involved in his first football row. Bert Herdman dropped him after a run of twenty-seven games in the first eleven, wisely believing Baxter, still thin, needed a rest.

But Jim didn't agree.

'He was livid,' Bert said afterwards. 'He asked me: "Are you daft, man? Ye canna drap me. I'm too good. I've got to play." '

That was the Baxter of yesterday—and it's still the Baxter of today, a man with tremendous faith in his own ability.

Herdman had more sense than other officials with whom Jim Baxter has tangled since. He just laughed. 'What a cheek that kid has, I thought. But I chuckled just the same. I knew a boy with such guts would go far. Aye, he's strong-headed, all right, but he knows what he wants. He won't be trampled on. He has guid Fife independence.'

It wasn't long until Baxter was back in the first team and he was the idol of the Raith fans, the greatest player Rovers had seen since Alex James. If Jim had the skill of Alex, he had different ideas about dress.

He refused to play in the long pants favoured by the club, even brought along a pair of his own. There was nothing for it—Bert Herdman ordered a special pair for Jim. He knew the time was coming when he could hold on to his brilliant wing-half no longer.

Now everyone was talking about Jim and he had played in an Under-23 international against Wales and he was ready for richer football fields.

Still English clubs shook their heads. They liked his play but they didn't think his physique was right. Herdman recalled: 'The boy was all skin and bone. The English clubs were doubtful, although they realised he had football intelligence rarely found in one so young.'

Then Rangers stepped in and bought Baxter for £17,500 in April 1960.

Baxter had arrived at last.

The international honours fell on him thick and fast. The legions of Rangers supporters licked their lips over Baxter's play, laughed at his antics and made him their greatest hero since Alan Morton.

Jim loved it, and put the seal on his career in 1963, the year of Baxter's Wembley, when he scored two goals for

Scotland in his first appearance at the great London stadium and made himself the prince of footballers.

Tragedy, alas, walks hand in hand with triumph in football.

Baxter was at the height of his success with Scotland and Rangers when he broke his leg playing against Vienna Rapid in Austria.

He had been playing brilliant football and it was due in no small measure to Baxter that Rangers, at last, were playing stylishly, playing football that had the foreigners afraid, playing with a confidence that made us believe they had a real chance of winning the European Cup.

But for Baxter the Ibrox saga was over. He was disenchanted with Rangers. He sought greener fields. When he came back after his severe injury he couldn't find his old form.

He was transferred to Sunderland in May 1965 for £70,000.

At Roker Park he has never been the hero he was at Ibrox, but the touches are still there and he showed against Brazil at Hampden in 1966 that he is still one of the most delightful footballers in the world, a breathtaking artist. I have no doubt that many more honours await Baxter, the gay spark, the man who can never be glum for long.

What is the real truth about Baxter? Is it true he thinks he knows it all, won't take advice and has been said to have yawned when a manager was giving the team a tactics talk?

Baxter has supreme faith in himself and certainly he cannot tolerate fools in football. Listen to Willie McNaught, former Scotland back, with whom Baxter played at Starks Park.

'It's nonsense to say that Jim Baxter won't take advice. I've never seen him turn up his nose at anything he was told by people who knew football.

'But I believe that if some director who had never kicked

a ball in his life tried to tell him what to do he'd walk away and ignore him.

'Anyhow, a man with such talent must have a mind of his own. He amazed me the first time I saw him play in the Rovers' reserve team. I had never seen anyone so young with so much polish and football sophistication. He was born with great skill but I feel he has absorbed a lot of knowledge since then.'

Baxter, of course, hasn't always been right and there will always be arguments about whether he and Denis Law should be played together in the same Scottish team. Some people feel they have so much talent that they subconsciously try to outdo each other.

One of his boyhood pals once told me: 'Jim's as bold as brass, but a great friend to have—a great bloke to have on your side.'

And colleagues have a high regard for Baxter. This is what wee Willie Henderson, the Rangers international winger, thinks: 'He's fabulous. Even when he plays a stinker, and that's not very often, he is as chirpy as when he is playing a stormer.

'His usual crack when he is playing wee is: "Don't give me the ball today, boys. I've no confidence." But there's no side with Jim. He never changes. He'd be the same if he met the Queen.'

It may be that Jim Baxter is too much of an extrovert for some critics' tastes. He is inclined, I know, to go over the score. But he usually has a laugh afterwards and says frankly: 'I'm a mug. I should keep my big mouth shut.'

His attitude towards referees is hardly a model for up-and-coming players. And not so long ago a reporter said this in his newspaper: 'The referee spoke to Jim Baxter half a dozen times, almost as many times as Jim ticked off the referee.'

But that is the weakness of so many real stars, of players

richly gifted as Baxter is: they hate to see their best work spoiled by what they think is an unfair decision, a lackadaisical move by a colleague or a foul by an opponent. So they talk —and talk.

They wouldn't, of course, be the great players they are if they kept as quiet as the functionally efficient usually do.

Anyhow, I have the feeling that Jim Baxter will be on the football scene for a long time yet. There is no player I'd sooner watch than Jim, who evokes the magic of the past with the sweetest passes seen since the days of Jimmy McMullan and who brings distinction and audacity to modern patterns.

And he is the one player of this era of whom it will be said fifty years from now: 'Aye, but you should have seen Jim Baxter . . . there's never been an artist like him.'

11

Soldier of Fortune

HEROES and heroics have gone out of fashion. In a world in which instinctive action is abhorred, the advent of a new D'Artagnan, Brigadier Gerard or Scarlet Pimpernel would be greeted with embarrassment, not cheers. This is the age of the anti-hero, the man who is human, not god-like, and whose patriotism or idealism is tinged with everyday ruthlessness, cynicism and vice. There's Bond, the savage sophisticate who started the new trend. There's Boysie, the liquidator with the cowardly streak. Unlike the Greeks, who endowed their historical heroes with supernatural qualities and deeds, we cannot protect our great men from destructive analysis. Indeed, we don't want to; we want to think our heroes have our own unworthy qualities, their valour being merely an odd quirk.

And that's a pity; perhaps, indeed, the real source of many of the ills of the world today. For I believe, with Thomas Carlyle, that society is founded on hero-worship. Heroes bring colour and glamour to a dull society. If there are no heroes where is the incentive? What boy wants to be a dingy, impoverished spy? What lad seeks to be a cunning politician or avaricious businessman who reaches the peak by stealth and kniving? But, according to modern literature, these are the men who matter today, the anti-heroes.

I am glad, therefore, that although football nowadays has

become duller with the introduction of method play and an accent on defence the anti-hero hasn't yet been accepted as the principal character. It is true, alas, that, especially since the last World Cup, the wrecker, the man whose main job is to stop the opposition at all costs, has come to the fore—and has been too often hailed as the saviour of his side instead of being heartily hooted as a villain, the reception he would certainly have received in the old days. But the destroyer is not generally accepted for most of us do not really like our footballers to have the less admirable traits of a Bond.

We want our soccer stars to have the theatrical heroism of less sophisticated times. We want them to be men of red blood and impulsive action. We want them to be match-winners, men who, like Rob Roy or Robin Hood, defied overwhelming odds by sheer force of physique, skill and imagination and achieved the seemingly impossible.

And in Denis Law, a slim, blond young man with a distinctive mop of whiffy hair, we have the footballing hero of heroes.

It is true that I have said at times that Law should not be included in the Scottish team and, by saying so, I have not endeared myself to Denis. But there were occasions when Law did not play to form in the blue shirt of his country and I felt someone who would think more about teamwork should fill his place.

Nevertheless, I have nothing but admiration for his football. He is a real master of his craft, one of the greatest forwards I have ever seen, a player who has already picked his place near the top in the game's hall of fame, and when he is at his best he has no peers in Britain, probably in the world.

If he has faults these are the faults of his impetuous nature, the failings of a Bulldog Drummond, not the studied, cruel revenges taken by a Bond. His reflexes are so fast, the fastest, probably, of any player of any time, that he is apt to lash out unthinkingly when he is fouled.

Perhaps, too, he is entitled to feel bitter when he is dropped by Scotland, usually on the grounds that he is too individualistic, too keen on playing his own way. For he can point to the fact that when he played for his country at the start he was involved in trouble . . . because he obeyed his orders to the letter.

In 1958, at eighteen, he became the youngest player to be capped for Scotland since R. S. McColl more than sixty years before. Against Ireland at Hampden, however, he did what he was told, forgot about his sheer football ability—and almost caused an international incident.

He was the terrier at the feet of the great Irishman Danny Blanchflower, and he worried and harried that star off his game.

Afterwards many people, not excluding the talkative Danny Blanchflower, thought Law had been too rough about his task.

Law said nothing; he seldom does. He may be an extrovert on the field but he likes to forget about football when he's at home. He truly wants, as he says, 'a quiet life'.

I believe, however, that Law was sickened by the outcry, upset because he was blamed so much. He did not play his natural game; he did not get a chance to play; he played as he was told to play; all he did was obey instructions. No wonder he shrugged later when he was accused by critics for not conforming to team plans made for the Scotland eleven.

Yet even Denis cannot deny that at times in the not-too-distant past he was a much more turbulent character, far too turbulent indeed, than he is today as the idol of thousands of Scottish and Manchester United fans. How could Denis help that? He was a combination of Billy Steel in his play and in pop star Tommy Steele in appearance. That didn't make for the peaceful soccer life.

And, like so many other great Scottish players, he had to show how good he was, to show that a puny physique as a lad was no handicap to a skilled and ambitious soccer player.

Even at eighteen Law was a long jump from the small, thin, fifteen-year-old boy sent from Aberdeen to Huddersfield to begin a football apprenticeship. He had been spotted by the brother of manager Andrew Beattie playing for Powis School. But when he arrived at Huddersfield station the waiting officials didn't recognise him. No wonder. He looked too frail to be a footballer—and he wore thick glasses to correct a squint.

Today, of course, the spectacles have gone, Law is a superb athlete, and the rough edges have been taken off, although Denis still isn't a player to turn the other cheek when hurt or insulted.

It took a long time, though, for Denis to realise that control meant much in football, that he couldn't sit back as he liked.

And, I think, it was in Italy that Law learned the value of discipline.

It was once the ambition of every young Scottish footballer to play for Celtic or Rangers, Hibernian or Hearts, Kilmarnock or Dundee, Aberdeen or Dunfermline. Now the face of football has changed and broader horizons beckon young men with twinkling feet. There is the promise of wealth in England. And for the more adventurous and more talented there is the dream of wealth to be found abroad.

In days of old, when Scotland was poor and the living bleak, our young men with spirit became the world's most famous soldiers of fortune, selling their swords to the highest bidder, fighting with a dedication and courage and skill that sent a shiver of panic down the backs of enemies. No doubt, centuries ago, the kings of Europe sent agents to tempt to their service the lustiest Scots.

And now, in the middle of the twentieth century, our footballers are being wooed by the Continent, although it is true that foreign governments have put their feet down to stop valuable currency being spent on players from other countries and salaries paid by many British clubs are big enough to keep stars at home.

I have no doubt, however, that if any Britisher were good enough and really wanted by an Italian or Spanish club the fee would be fabulous—and the money would be found, despite current—and currency—difficulties.

Anyhow, only a few years ago, Italy, with the wealthiest clubs in the world, were desperately keen on Scots. And the man every young Scot with talent and ambition wanted to meet was Gigi Peronace.

The smiling Italian was a super scout, symbolising the amazing change in football deals.

He might have stepped out of an advertisement for the International Look of the 1960's. He was brisk, suave, with the smiling personality of a Mario Lanza. He dressed in sober blue—but the immaculate cut was Roman. His tie was rich red and black, effulgent as a tapestry from Florence. He spent most of his life in plush hotels, bustling airports and speeding trains.

A more vivid contrast could not be imagined than that of Gigi Peronace with the old-time scout, serge-suited, cap square on forehead, lurking around broken-down pavilions, worrying over every penny he could spend on a transfer.

Peronace was the new status symbol of the modern, dazzling, money-drenched world of international football. Then he was 'business director' of Turin, planning the policy for new players with the club's board, organising glamour matches abroad. He could offer a film star's salary to the players he wanted.

And only those few years ago, Gigi, unlike his counterparts of the 'twenties and 'thirties, didn't have to stalk the men he sought. Players with stars in their eyes, hope of untold money in the bank and dreams of sunny Italy in their hearts were only too glad to meet the dark-eyed, voluble Italian with the perfect English accent, the personality who could transport them to the glittering heights of success, to luxury flats, servants, expensive sports cars, the adulation of enthusiastic Italian football fans.

Peronace, who gave up university classes for football when he was studying to be an aircraft engineer, travelled the world to keep up to date with modern trends and to note the names of players who might suit his club, Turino.

He once told me: 'You could say we are like your Rangers. We have always been a fighting side, playing hard football.'

That is why he was so keen to get Denis Law, who had been transferred from Huddersfield Town to Manchester City in 1960 for a then record fee of £55,000.

Persuasive Gigi got his man—at a fee reckoned to be around £100,000.

And Italy changed Law. He loved the brassy sun, the passionate fervour of football in a torrid land, the colour and the drama and the high-powered living in Italy. And that, I believe, is why Denis Law blossomed from a brilliant but often eccentric, moody and 'individual' player into the man hailed in 1962 as the greatest inside-forward in the world—a forward with the speed of a gazelle, the striking power of a barracuda.

At that time Law craved colour. The frail, bespectacled schoolboy from rugged Scotland had always longed for adventure in an exotic setting.

So he became the idol of Turin, the dashing Scottish soldier of fortune, whose dramatic personality, flossy mop of blond hair and bronzed, handsome features fitted perfectly into the Latin way of life.

Law became the new Law, Law the dedicated footballer, because he has always taken life as a challenge. He might have been a successful soldier if he hadn't been a soccer star.

His accent to this day is that of a veteran Scottish regular, the lilt of his native north intertwined with a trace of Yorkshire, a spice Lancashire and laced with many a foreign phrase.

He had no homesickness. He knew what it was to venture far from home. As he said at the time:

'I left Aberdeen at fifteen to go to England. I was lucky right away. My landlady treated me like a son. Since then I've never worried about being away. But it is only since I went to Italy that I developed into a seasoned footballer.'

Once, in his villa outside Turin, Law, casually debonair in Italian-line suit, thought back to less happy days, to his nightmare at Wembley when he played against England and dismayed his friends with a show of petulance. He explained frankly:

'It was only when I came to Italy that I began to realise I hadn't grown up. For example, it's childish to kick the ball away. I learned quickly here in Italy. Officials and referees just won't tolerate any trouble. Why should they? We players are paid fabulously. We should do our jobs like men.'

That is Law the sensible speaking. There you find again the trace of the soldier. It has always seemed to me that the top-class player would do well in the army. In my travels abroad with Scottish teams this has become obvious to me. At home people are puzzled because such-and-such a star, so brilliant on his native soil, has failed on tours. It is a matter of temperament, of spirit.

Those stars who fail in strange lands may be just as clever as the players who succeed, but they lack the heart and the discipline of what I may call the stout regular, the backbone of the army and of the game of football.

It wasn't easy for a British player to live in Italy, for it takes time to get used to the food, the sun, the language, the Latin temperament.

For a spell Law succeeded. And he admits now that his sojourn in the sun did him good, probably made him great. He had to cut out temperamental frills.

But Law never became the perfect Italian footballer. How could he?

No Briton can. I'm convinced of that. It is not in the British make-up to become a hermit. That's the role of the Italian soccer star.

Law tried. But even after heart-searching discussions with himself about his failings he could never attain the self-discipline of a militant monk. 'That's what the Italians want you to be,' he once said. 'But I just couldn't. I don't think any Briton could.'

Although the fans idolised him, disillusionment with Italy set in. Peronace said sadly: 'It was a pity. Law had become truly great. But I always knew that. I was determined to get him for Torino. I put him when I first saw him above even Johnny Haynes or Greaves. I was right. I knew he had faults. But I liked his fighting spirit. Alas, he cannot be tamed, held captive by one club.'

Law came back to Britain, to Manchester. This time his new club was Manchester United and manager Matt Busby paid a record £116,000 for Law in July 1962. 'It was still a bargain,' says Matt quietly.

Today Law is quieter than of yore. But he is still outspoken. He likes others to be outspoken as well. There was, for instance, the argument he had with Manchester City when he played for that club.

Law says: 'The season we were threatened with relegation I made it plain that I didn't fancy playing in Second Division football.' He grinned. 'At once, our chairman, Mr. Alan Douglas, snapped: "If Law doesn't fancy it here, he can go." Well, I liked that. I really did. I like a guy who calls a spade a spade. And I told Mr. Douglas: "Look here, boss, we're not in the Second Division. And if I have my way we won't be. And we weren't.'

Law is not always the reporter's friend. That's because he doesn't comment on matches. Maybe he's right. For he once said shrewdly: 'See these reporters? How can they always be right? They've got to sum up in a few minutes what it would take a High Court judge weeks to consider before giving a verdict.' That, Mr. Law, is a point.

Law could be called the complete cosmopolitan, the international man of the world, the character of distinction you glimpse at the great airports of Europe. But always, at heart, he is the fervent Scot. 'The dark blue shirt of Scotland does something for me,' he admits.

And perhaps that is why he is so upset when critics like myself say he should not be picked for Scotland. He is still desperately keen to turn out for his country and if he has not always played to the plan and ignored his partners it is probably because he is so eager for Scotland to win that, subconsciously, he has done what he thinks is right, even though the planners don't agree. And, in truth, who is really to say that Denis Law, superb footballer, is wrong?

Yet Law never makes excuses when he is criticised. He usually shrugs, shakes his head—or glares—and walks away.

But away from the football field Law is a character, a smiling lad with a fine sense of humour, never out of sorts as other stars can be.

How good a player is Law? At his best there is no one superior to him in the world as an inspiration, a scorer, a saver of forlorn hopes. There is an electric touch about his play. He is not a Scottish inside-forward of the old school. There is nothing dainty, scheming, cunning, cultured, leisurely about Law.

His reflexes are superb. His swerve is stupendous, his acceleration breathtaking. And there is no forward in the world today who can rise in the air like Law. He is a man's man, a footballing hero out for death or glory, tremendously gifted athletically.

But his brain ticks over just like any great old-timer's. So he has the best of two worlds—the world of the thinker and the world of the striker.

Some say Denis Law cannot last in football until a ripe old age. I'm not so sure. He has never been given enough credit for his football *thought*; he has invariably been acclaimed for his *action*, more dramatic, more forceful, more effective than that of any British forward I have ever known.

But Law thinks, as well. And now that he has settled to happy married life in Manchester, now his hair-trigger temper is more controlled, the best days for Denis Law may lie ahead, not behind.

For he is a player who has always taken lessons to heart.

Mr. Big

ARGUMENTS still rage as to whether George Young was a better centre-half than Willie Woodburn. Woodburn was more incisive in the tackle, say some. Ah, but Young was more commanding, declare others. All I'll say about this controversy is that Young and Woodburn, the giants of Rangers in one of the club's most spectacular eras, were the two best centre-halves I ever saw. I'll go further: they were the two best centre-halves the world has ever known, both far superior to anyone, at home or abroad, at a time, too, when outstanding players, English, Irish and foreign, filled this position.

But I have no hesitation in naming George Young as football's most magnificent defender, the master craftsman of rearguard strategy.

He was football's Mr. Big in every respect—an inspiring captain of Scotland and Rangers, a brilliant tactician, a glowing example to aspiring footballers, an imaginative thinker and a man who gave everything he had to the game, who helped more than most to make football the lucrative and respected profession it is today and who was known as one of the cleanest and most sporting of athletes.

Some people still sneer that George Young was a lucky player, that he put too much emphasis on defence and asked for too much support from his wing-halves, whether he was playing at centre-half or right-back. That is nonsense. Young

was as good at back as he was at centre-half, which is why I
have listed him as my master of defence.

It is true his massive physique helped. But how many big
fellows in football have been failures? Too many. George
had more than a giant's build. He had an uncanny knack of
reading the game and his positional sense had a touch of
magic. No defender was more difficult to beat. And his kicking of the ball has never been surpassed for sheer efficiency.

Some critics decry Young's big punt and his central role
in Rangers' Iron Curtain defence. They don't look beyond
their noses. They don't realise even yet that Young had one of
football's best brains, that victory was his main aim, as it must
be of every great player and skipper, and that the technique
with which he was so intimately involved was used because it
was the most suitable for his teams and times. All you need
do is study the astounding list of successes which attended
Young and Rangers.

And Young's prodigious punt was not merely a happy-go-
lucky bash at the ball to get it out of danger. Most times the
ball landed at the feet of a forward. Young could, indeed,
pass the ball as accurately as an accomplished inside-forward.
I remember one of his colleagues, Willie Waddell, then at
the peak of his international form, telling me of Young: 'A
great thing about his play is that he can pass the ball along
the ground.' Oh, yes, Young could vary his play.

But when he was taken from the centre-half position and
played at right-back to make room for Willie Woodburn a
new Rangers policy was being perfected: the renowned Iron
Curtain, which became a defensive system without equal.

Some purists groaned. Rangers fans didn't. Rangers got
results.

They ignored the moves that had brought fame in the old
days to Scottish soccer—the short pass to half-back from back.

They relied on their defenders using a powerful punt into the opposition goal area, which allowed the Ibrox forwards to score goals in a smash-and-grab fashion, a fashion in which they were specialists.

Some critics had no liking for the area of fifty yards divided by the midfield line becoming a soccer Sahara, screamed that football was becoming too streamlined and deprived of beauty because of the disappearance of skilful approach work, the happy cohesion between the wing-halves and inside-forwards, the sudden burst down the line by the wingers.

They didn't appreciate there was skill in the accuracy of Young's lobs. It is much more difficult to kick the ball sixty yards and find a target than it is to slide it ten yards.

There are many ways of playing football. Now, as I've said, the method way is bringing complaints. In the early 'fifties the Iron Curtain plan was criticised. But the good player can shine in any system. Young would have been as outstanding in any role allotted him.

Not only did he stand out as Colossus, a man of incomparable individual talent, but he was a wonderful team man and, with Sammy Cox, also of Rangers, he made up the best full-back partnership in Scottish football history.

As a team these two were far better than any other pair I've seen, even though there may have been more spectacular individualists, and in their play they allied the best of two worlds of backs—the old world in which defenders were men of redoubtable physique noted more for their fearless tackling and lusty clearances than for artistry and the new world in which backs are usually little men who prefer a pass to a full-blooded kick and who could more rightly be named auxiliary wing-halves.

Those who were lucky enough to see Young play with Cox for Scotland will know that it is nonsense to insist that Young always wanted to pump the ball long and high out of danger. His tactics depended on the type of players available and I have seen George Young at Wembley and Hampden, Ninian and Windsor Parks, and many a foreign stadium, use a delicacy of soccer touch that was amazing in one so big—a style in complete contrast to that so often in evidence at Ibrox. If he thought it was called for, George could slip the ball to his wing-half or inside-forward as neatly as anyone.

Another feature of the play of Young and Cox was their commendable caution, a quality in full-backs which, alas, is not at all prevalent today. Frankly, I do not relish international defenders taking dare-devil risks in a Scottish team. Certainly no one since has had such an air of invincibility as Young and Cox.

Young looked as imperturbable as Ailsa Craig—and was. His bulk was reassuring. You felt that here was everything in Scotland that was dependable. Cox was all wire, a crackling whip of a player who tackled devastatingly. He was fast, slick and elusive, one of the most versatile stars ever to appear on a football field.

Indeed, I feel Young was the man most instrumental in making defence almost an art. After the war, defence improved out of recognition. A good thing? Some still complain and, when the Iron Curtains were introduced in the late 'forties and early 'fifties, fans sighed in exasperation as the accent was all on defence with the instructions: grab a goal and defend for the rest of the game.

But it must be admitted success was achieved by many and certainly defence in modern times has been brought to a far finer, tighter art than it ever was in the old days.

Young was a man of his age. I cannot name a player who has given more sustained effort and enthusiasm to club and country than George Young. Controversy enveloped him but he could never be accused of being a selfish player. It wasn't entirely his wish that the long punt became his trademark, for, as I've pointed out, he was an undoubtedly skilful player and could keep the ball on the deck with more accuracy than most.

Now, however, there is still no more illustrious name in football than that of Young, who will never be forgotten.

How Scotland could do with a Young in command today! His enthusiasm was infectious. I believe he would have laid his life down for Scotland. I once asked him what his biggest kick had been. He told me:

'Well, it wasn't a goal scored or a goal averted or anything like that. It was at Wembley in 1949. That year the teams came on to the field from the far end of the ground opposite the old entrance. My eye caught sight of the scoreboard with just two words on it: ENGLAND   SCOTLAND.

'I had never noticed it before. I got a queer feeling, a wee tremor at the heart, and through my mind the thought passed, what will be on it at the finish?

'But then things happened—the usual Wembley ceremonial, standing to attention, the band playing the National Anthem, the line-up, the referee's whistle and away we went.

'It was a good game for us. Jimmy Cowan saw to that for a start. At a breathing space in the second half Jimmy said to me: "We're all right, George." We were all feeling very pleased with ourselves. At any rate, I know I was.

'I had forgotten ever having noticed the scoreboard, but something I couldn't explain caused me to look for it and this is what I saw'; ENGLAND 0 SCOTLAND 3.

'I had seen Jimmy Mason, Billy Steel and Lawrie Reilly score their goals, but the sight of these figures brought a full realisation of what we had accomplished and a glow of delight ran through me. I could feel the old heart jump for joy.

'We were winning at Wembley. I was captain of a grand bunch of lads who were bringing back the international trophy at last, after thirteeen years.

'This was my big kick. I had never before felt such a feeling of elation and I have never felt it since. The board altered to 1—3 before the finish, but that didn't matter. I had got my great big thrill on my most memorable day.'

That's the real George Young, a great skipper, a great player, an unpretentious man for all his success, never a big-head, Scotland-daft.

George has said he is not a superstitious man, for he believed that good football, not good luck, was the essence of success. Yet his nickname was 'Corky' and it was bestowed on him because he became the owner of one of football's most famous lucky charms.

After Rangers had won the Scottish Cup in 1948 the trophy was filled with champagne at the banquet which followed the final. After the first bottle had been opened the waiter handed Young the cork and said: 'This will bring you luck.' George decided to give it a trial. And it worked.

In October 1948 Scotland beat Wales at Cardiff to register their first post-war victory in a full international—and luck was with Young and his boys. In November fortune was again with skipper Young when the Scots beat Ireland at Hampden. Then came the vital match, the Wembley clash with England in April.

One of George's most important tasks before he left home was to place Scotland's lucky cork in his blazer pocket. At the team's hotel in Surrey another waiter presented Young with a lucky silver dollar. George put the dollar beside the cork—and wondered if he were being foolish.

But Scotland won, thanks mainly to the inspired goalkeep-

ing of Jimmy Cowan—and Scotland had at last won the home
international championship.

And the famous cork became a legend.

It is said that luck played a part in Young's signing for
Rangers. This is the story:

An athlete named Stirling had his eye on a boxing title
and he asked Falkirk if he could train at Brockville. He was
given permission and enjoyed training so much that he gave
up boxing in favour of football. He became a goalkeeper and
was given a trial for Kirkintilloch Rob Roy, the famous junior
club.

He told the junior officials he knew of a good full-back—
'A great big fellow'—who played in a team at Grangemouth.
The back's name was George Young and within a month
George was booked for Rangers . . . the start of a tremendous
soccer saga, for Young stayed in the Ibrox first team for seventeen years, won every honour in Scotland and gained eighty
international caps.

I don't believe luck had anything to do with it: Young was
a natural, such a brilliant player even as a youngster that he
would undoubtedly have risen to the top even if he had been
cursed with ill fortune.

He was born in Grangemouth in 1922 and when he was
nine he was chosen for his school team. Soon, as a defender,
of course, he was playing for Scotland's schoolboys, in the
same team as Billy Steel, who became his friend. Small Billy
and tall George were known as 'Mutt and Jeff'.

When he joined Rob Roy, Young was a left-back—and that
was his position in Rangers' reserve side, whom he joined in
1941. But he never played in that position for the first eleven.
He was invariably right-back or centre-half—and what a barrier the big fellow of 6 ft. $1\frac{1}{2}$ in. and fourteen stones proved
to be over the years for Rangers.

I

When George decided to retire in 1957 his decision stunned the fans. But he was thirty-five and he decided to go when he was still at the top.

No footballer's life, however, is roses, roses all the way—not even that of George Young. And he received what I felt was an unnecessary humiliation just before he retired.

He had been looked on for years by younger players not only as an inspiring skipper but a friend and adviser. In the eyes of many he was unofficial team manager of Scotland.

No one had given such loyal service as Young, without ever a moan. His nose had been broken three times. He'd had more than fifty stitches sewn into various parts of his body. His legs had been in plaster six times. A finger had been broken in an international.

He never complained—but never was he so badly hurt as when he was dropped from the Scottish World Cup team to play Spain in Madrid in June 1957.

When the team left for a Continental tour George was with them, hopeful that he would lead Scotland into the World Cup finals. He wanted to say farewell to soccer in the game against Spain in Madrid.

Why not? He had played valiantly in the qualifying matches against Spain in Scotland and Switzerland in Basle. Indeed, Young's tactics had won the day in Basle. And now Scotland had only to draw in Spain to make certain of taking part in the World Cup finals, to be played in Sweden in 1958.

But Young was dropped—Young the man who had played for Scotland more than anyone else. And without a word of explanation or sympathy.

That, indeed, was a black day for Scottish football.

Young is too big a man to bear grudges, however. The gentle giant now is in business and writes a newspaper column. He had a spell as manager with Third Lanark and it seems a great pity to me that a man of such football knowledge, experience, sympathy, personality and tactical ability is not in a key position in the game to which he gave such distinguished service.

He was Scotland's greatest captain.

13

Those I have Missed

WHEN you look back down memory lane you realise what a magnificent contribution Scotland has made to football. No country has given more masters to soccer. No country has had such a wealth of cultured, imaginative players. Indeed, when I study the list of players I have chosen as my great masters I am embarrassed and I know there will be an outcry even from the most placid of my readers. Not without cause.

But I stress again that this is a personal choice. And who can ever be right in a selection like this!

I am merely a football reporter. After all, such a wonderful player as Patsy Gallacher was once assailed by indignant readers when he dared to name in a Sunday paper the finest eleven players he had known. I recall him smiling as he said: 'There was one letter that made me blink. It said: "I don't know why you could have become such a great player when it is obvious you know nothing about football. The team you have said would have been the greatest wouldn't have won the Scottish Junior Cup." '

I am inclined to agree with Patsy's view, however, that all of us who dare to choose a team of the greatest of the great are inclined to overload it with old-timers. Not without cause, though. As Patsy said, the old-timers live more vividly in the memory of those of us who are no longer young; perhaps because in the golden days the money angle was not so heavily emphasised or perhaps because discipline was not so strict then as now.

Certainly the players of the past seemed more colourful.

There was the peerless Bobby Walker, father of Scottish inside-forward play, who was an example of the fact that there was more fun in soccer in the old days.

Can you imagine a player on an international trip today being photographed—as the world heavyweight champion? Bobby Walker was. In Dublin with a Scotland team at the same time as the boxing champion, Tommy Burns, was there, Bobby dropped into a bar with team-mate Charlie Thomson. The proprietor got it into his Irish head that Walker was Burns and Charlie kept up the joke. A photographer was sent for and Walker told all the customers just how he was going to win his next big fight.

And can you imagine a player of today laying the referee low, then refusing to leave the field? It happened. One of the greatest wing-halves of all time, Sunny Jim Young, was playing for Celtic in Berlin against Burnley for a challenge cup put up by the Germans. When the referee trotted on to the field his strip closely resembled the Burnley outfit. Celtic players asked him to change. Curtly, he declined. Which was a mistake—by the referee, who certainly didn't know Sunny Jim.

Early in the game the ball landed near him. Before he could move . . . Crash! Sunny had tackled him at full power. The poor referee must have thought the stand had fallen on him.

When he regained his breath he ordered Young off. Sunny Jim protested. It was all an innocent mistake, he said blandly; he thought, in the heat of the moment, that the referee was a Burnley player.

So the referee ran off to change his jersey, Young remaining on the pitch—the picture of injured innocence.

Incidentally, the team Patsy Gallacher named as the best was: Brownlie (Third Lanark); McNair and Dodds (both Celtic); Young (Celtic), Raisbeck (Partick Thistle), McMullan (Partick Thistle); Archibald and Cunningham (both Rangers), Quinn (Celtic), McAlpine (Queen's Park) and Morton (Rangers).

Patsy was criticised by many for leaving out other greats, but, after all, this was chosen as his best team. And I must make it clear that the players I have chosen as masters would not necessarily make the most outstanding side. I have picked my men as the masters in their own particular positions.

I wouldn't necessarily have chosen them if I had been selecting the best-blended eleven.

For instance, take wing play. Gordon Smith is my nomination. But in international football Willie Waddell would have been my selection, especially if Jimmy Mason had been the inside-right.

What a brilliant combination these two were: Mason the shrewd passer and Waddell the terror of the touchline, sparks flying from his studs as he pelted down the wing.

And there was the classic partnership of George Stevenson and Bobby Ferrier, the pride of Motherwell. Oh yes, they were fine individualists but it was as a pair that they earned undying fame.

In selecting a team, blend is the thing. Patsy Gallacher made this clear when he was talking about full-backs, for instance. My choice would be Young and Cox, of Scotland and Rangers. Patsy's was McNair and Dodds, of Celtic.

He said: 'If the full-backs are to be taken as a partnership I don't think McNair and Dodds can be bettered. Even if the individual selection is made, McNair must be the choice for his coolness and perfect positioning. He made his head save

his legs to the extent that sometimes one would think he had
hypnotised his opponent into parting with the ball.

'His only rival would be Billy McCracken, who was an
offside specialist and when he had sprung his trap his shout
of "Offside, ref" made the sparrows in the stand roof flutter.

'And there was another Irishman well known in Scotland,
Billy McCandless. But McNair and McCandless would never
have made a good partnership, since their methods were too
similar, but, given a dashing right-back, Billy was ideal.'

In my own selection I must point out that my head has
ruled my heart. It is one of the most pleasing aspects of football that players steal a place for ever in your heart although
they may not be of world class because, being Scots, they just
cannot be bad players and are endowed with a native skill that
would have brought them much more fame had they gone to
England.

I cannot, for instance, ever forget Jimmy Williamson, who
played for Kilmarnock and Partick Thistle. Here was a real
artist, a man of great skill who, in an era less rich in superb
inside-forward talent, would have received constant international recognition.

And I was reluctant to pass over the claims to be a supreme
master of Alec Jackson, of Aberdeen, Huddersfield Town
and Chelsea, the smiling man with the film-star profile, whose
tremendous speed and powerful shot won scores of games.
The right-winger with the gazelle's grace became a national
figure in the days when football didn't have television to make
players world-famous.

Peter McKennan, too, has his admirers. Only Partick
Thistle, the mercurial team which topples the mighty one
Saturday and flops to weak opposition the next, could have
produced a character like Peter, known as 'Ma Ba' '. He could
make the ball sit up and beg—but he had more than magic

ball control to give him a place in the gallery of greats, for on his day there were few better inside-forwards. He could shoot like Billy Liddell, his moves were spiced with dashes of Matthews's foot fantasy and he had the defence-breaking guile of Peter Doherty.

All these players I loved to watch—all these and many more: George Hamilton, Aberdeen's dapper attacker, Charlie Tully, Celtic's Irish bag o' tricks, Willie Fernie, another wizard of Parkhead, Bobby Collins, whose courage was phenomenal, Willie Thornton, most thoughtful Rangers centre-forward, Adam Little, distinguished wing-half, also of Rangers, Jock McEwan, a Kilmarnock half-back who never received the international recognition that was his due, Bob Gillespie, Queen's Park centre-half, Alec Troup, of Dundee, and the brilliant Tommy Walker, of Hearts. Ah, but the list is endless.

Perhaps they could rightly be called great masters. It is not for me to say they were not. What I have tried to do is select, on merit and without bias as to club, the men I believe most deserve the title.

There are many I have missed, I know. And it is at centre-forward that I am most perturbed. Hughie Gallacher is my choice—but was he so much better than Jimmy McGrory or Lawrie Reilly?

I must pay tribute here to two leaders who gave me some of my most memorable football memories.

There is no doubt that Jimmy McGrory, of Celtic, was the greatest header of a ball football has known and I can see him yet, leaping high in the air, twisting his powerful neck and flicking the ball as fiercely with his head as most forwards could with their feet past a helpless goalkeeper. It is true that McGrory played in Celtic's golden age and was fortunate that he had as colleagues some of the most bewildering ball-workers of all time. Yet without McGrory's dash, urge, power, shooting and, above all, heading ability the great Celtic teams in which he played would not have been complete units.

There was nothing subtle about his methods. He had the physical attributes and the power to score goals. That was his job and he did it supremely well.

Perhaps, however, it is because there are few like McGrory today that method play has emerged. But why make football more difficult? The aim of the game is to get the ball into the back of the net as often as possible. That's what centre-forwards are for, to score goals.

If the modern leaders, like McGrory, developed their talents on the old-fashioned lines of shooting and heading whenever a chance appeared there would be much more excitement in the game nowadays.

It is true that some clubs, even those obsessed by method, have been trying to find a leader who will employ the old battering-ram tactics. But it seems to me that rigid pattern play and an old-fashioned leader won't blend. The old flamboyant centre-forwards needed wingers who could cross accurately, and needed, too, long balls through the centre on to which they could pounce. I am not against clubs trying to put drama into a game that has become stereotyped, but I feel they are being too clever in attempting to mould the old with the new.

Still, if we could find a new Lawrie Reilly . . . that would be different. Reilly was the perfect mixture of the old and the new. Last-minute Reilly, they called him—a name which might have suited a rooting, tooting cowboy, quick on the draw and deadly on the target. Reilly was no cowboy, but he was slick on the draw and seldom off the target. Not only could he score goals in the old, spectacular McGrory way; he led his line brilliantly; in his play you found glimpses of all the great leaders, not only the dash of McGrory but the sub-tlety of Gallacher and the shooting power of Andy Wilson; and he could vary his play in a way which would have brought a smile to the faces of managers who favour method play.

He could be effective, this brilliant Hibernian player, whether he was leading his forwards from behind in the Revie manner, making use of orthodox wingers, combining skil-fully with cultured inside-forwards, or simply leading the line in the best way of all—the old-fashioned way and the way Reilly loved best : by distributing play neatly, then speed-ing on, right to the front of the attack, to finish off the raids.

He earned his nickname because of the astonishing number of dramatic last-minute goals he scored for Scotland and Hibernian. What was the secret? Reilly put his finger on it—and gave a lead to clubs who are wondering why they fail so badly—when he once told me :

'Most of my last-minute goals came in internationals and it is rather strange that most of these goals were equalisers. But I was honoured to play in any team which gave me the chance to score last-minute goals because, in such a side, one was playing with colleagues who were prepared to go for the full ninety minutes.'

Would Reilly have reached the stars if he hadn't been play-ing in such an outstanding attack as the Hibernian line of Smith, Johnstone, Reilly, Turnbull and Ormond?

I think he would.

It was not without deep thought, either, that I left out of my list David Meiklejohn, of Rangers, Bobby Evans, of Cel-tic, and Jimmy McMullan, of Thistle and Manchester City.

If these three had played together they would probably have gone down in history as the most accomplished half-back line of any country.

Evans may not have been one of the silkiest players I have

seen, lacking the touches of a George Brown, for instance, but to see this fighting red-head storm into attacking action, drumming on relentlessly his colleagues in front, was like watching a tournament at an ancient court, with Evans the scarlet knight, the hero of the joust.

There was pageantry and pomp and panoply about Bobby Evans. He reminded me of a clan chief, a spectacular attacker who could rally faltering comrades with his clarion call. He may have been too touchy, sometimes temperamental, but only off the field, and he gave all, as he still, astonishingly, does for Raith Rovers, and expected all from everyone else.

Rangers fans may disagree with me when I say I think Young and Woodburn were their greatest centre-halves. What about David Meiklejohn, the veterans will demand? Certainly Davie was one of the giants of football, one of the most versatile half-backs of all times. He had the presence of a Young, tremendous strength and stamina and skill to match. His generalship was superb and invariably he was in the right place at the right time. No man ever took his football so seriously. No playboy approach by 'Meek', no time for jokes, no thoughts that 'this is only a game'. Football was life to Meiklejohn and about his play and captaincy were the fervour, single-mindedness and urge of an old-time preacher. No man was more capable of putting backbone into a football team than Meiklejohn, whose best position, in my opinion, was centre-half.

In vivid contrast to Evans was Jimmy McMullan, yet another great Scottish captain. He was a model to modern winghalves who prefer the delicate touch to powerful grafting. McMullan stroked the ball, patted it, caressed it, nursed it with velvet toe. His passes were perfection. His positional play was uncanny.

Who else have I missed? Scores, alas. But you can't nominate everyone.

Perhaps Bob McPhail and Andy Cunningham, those power-house inside-forwards of Rangers who gave a new look to Scottish football, should have been named. I know admirers of Jerry Dawson will be upset because he is not chosen as the master of all goalkeepers and, to be fair, the inspiring Ranger was probably as talented as John Thomson. And voices from the distant football past whisper that Walter Arnott, of Queen's Park, who played for Scotland against England ten times, every year from 1884 to 1893, was the most accomplished full-back who ever took the field.

In the end, perhaps, there will be men playing today more deserving of the title 'master' than anyone I have named.

Even in this age of method their talent and natural ability will come shining through.

There are Willie Henderson, a winger of great merit, Ronnie McKinnon and Billy McNeill, commanding centre-halves, Pat Crerand, at his best a superb passer of the ball, and one or two more.

For me the happiest feature is that Scotland is still producing players entitled to be described as masters—and will always continue to do so.

For football is still our most loved sport.

Index